T0040459

PEPPERCANISTER POEMS 1972–1978

THOMAS KINSELLA

PEPPERCANISTER

POEMS

1972 - 1978

WAKE FOREST UNIVERSITY PRESS

This edition first published 1979
Reprinted 1986

Library of Congress Catalog Card No. 79-63669
ISBN 0-916390-10-x

CONTENTS

Peppercanister was established in 1972 as a small private publishing enterprise, with the purpose of issuing occasional special items from our home in Dublin, across the Grand Canal from St. Stephen's Church, known locally as 'The Peppercanister'.

The first series of Peppercanister publications consisted of four occasional poems : *Butcher's Dozen*, issued in April 1972 in response to the report of the Widgery Tribunal of Inquiry into the shooting of thirteen Civil Rights demonstrators by the British Army in Derry on 30 January 1972; *A Selected Life* and *Vertical Man*, two poems in memory of Seán O Riada, who died in October 1971 (these were issued in limited editions in 1972 and 1973 respectively); and *The Good Fight*, a poem for the tenth anniversary of the assassination of John F. Kennedy, issued in a limited edition on 22 November 1973.

A second series of three Peppercanister publications consisted of limited editions of two sequences — *One* (1974) and *A Technical Supplement* (1976), continuing the themes of *Notes from the Land of the Dead* — and a group of poems published in 1978 as *Song of the Night and Other Poems*. *The Messenger*, a poem written in memory of my father, was also issued in 1978.

All eight titles, with a commentary on the first four occasional poems, are collected in this volume.

*

The illustration on page 11 is the badge issued at the Civil Rights protest march in Newry a week after the Derry killings; on page 21 is a profile medallion of Seán O Riada based on the death mask made by the late sculptor Séamus Murphy;

[9]

on page 35 a portrait head of Plato in the National Museum, Athens; on page 51 a drawing by Anne Yeats; on page 73 a detail from one of the illustrations to Diderot's *Encyclopédie*; on page 97 a drawing by the author; and on page 117 the figure of Hermes/Mercurius.

T. K.

BUTCHER'S DOZEN

1972

BUTCHER'S DOZEN:
A LESSON FOR
THE OCTAVE OF WIDGERY

I went with Anger at my heel
Through Bogside of the bitter zeal
— Jesus pity! — on a day
Of cold and drizzle and decay.
A month had passed. Yet there remained
A murder smell that stung and stained.
On flats and alleys — over all —
It hung; on battered roof and wall,
On wreck and rubbish scattered thick,
On sullen steps and pitted brick.
And when I came where thirteen died
It shrivelled up my heart. I sighed
And looked about that brutal place
Of rage and terror and disgrace.
Then my moistened lips grew dry.
I had heard an answering sigh!
There in a ghostly pool of blood
A crumpled phantom hugged the mud:
'Once there lived a hooligan.
A pig came up, and away he ran.
Here lies one in blood and bones,
Who lost his life for throwing stones.'
More voices rose. I turned and saw
Three corpses forming, red and raw,
From dirt and stone. Each upturned face
Stared unseeing from its place:
'Behind this barrier, blighters three,
We scrambled back and made to flee.
The guns cried *Stop*, and here lie we.'

[13]

Then from left and right they came,
More mangled corpses, bleeding, lame,
Holding their wounds. They chose their ground,
Ghost by ghost, without a sound,
And one stepped forward, soiled and white :
'A bomber I. I travelled light
— Four pounds of nails and gelignite
About my person, hid so well
They seemed to vanish where I fell.
When the bullet stopped my breath
A doctor sought the cause of death.
He upped my shirt, undid my fly,
Twice he moved my limbs awry,
And noticed nothing. By and by
A soldier, with his sharper eye,
Beheld the four elusive rockets
Stuffed in my coat and trouser pockets.
Yes, they must be strict with us,
Even in death so treacherous !'
He faded, and another said :
'We three met close when we were dead.
Into an armoured car they piled us
Where our mingled blood defiled us,
Certain, if not dead before,
To suffocate upon the floor.
Careful bullets in the back
Stopped our terrorist attack,
And so three dangerous lives are done
— Judged, condemned and shamed in one.'
That spectre faded in his turn.
A harsher stirred, and spoke in scorn :
'The shame is theirs, in word and deed,
Who prate of Justice, practise greed,

And act in ignorant fury — then,
Officers and gentlemen,
Send to their Courts for the Most High
To tell us did we really die!
Does it need recourse to law
To tell ten thousand what they saw?
Law that lets them, caught red-handed,
Halt the game and leave it stranded,
Summon up a sworn inquiry
And dump their conscience in the diary.
During which hiatus, should
Their legal basis vanish, good,
The thing is rapidly arranged:
Where's the law that can't be changed?
The news is out. The troops were kind.
Impartial justice has to find
We'd be alive and well today
If we had let them have their way.
Yet England, even as you lie,
You give the facts that you deny.
Spread the lie with all your power
— All that's left; it's turning sour.
Friend and stranger, bride and brother,
Son and sister, father, mother,
All not blinded by your smoke,
Photographers who caught your stroke,
The priests that blessed our bodies, spoke
And wagged our blood in the world's face.
The truth will out, to your disgrace.'
He flushed and faded. Pale and grim,
A joking spectre followed him:
'Take a bunch of stunted shoots,
A tangle of transplanted roots,

[15]

Ropes and rifles, feathered nests,
Some dried colonial interests,
A hard unnatural union grown
In a bed of blood and bone,
Tongue of serpent, gut of hog
Spiced with spleen of underdog.
Stir in, with oaths of loyalty,
Sectarian supremacy,
And heat, to make a proper botch,
In a bouillon of bitter Scotch.
Last, the choice ingredient : you.
Now, to crown your Irish stew,
Boil it over, make a mess.
A most imperial success !'
He capered weakly, racked with pain,
His dead hair plastered in the rain :
The group was silent once again.
It seemed the moment to explain
That sympathetic politicians
Say our violent traditions,
Backward looks and bitterness
Keep us in this dire distress.
We must forget, and look ahead,
Nurse the living, not the dead.
My words died out. A phantom said :
'Here lies one who breathed his last
Firmly reminded of the past.
A trooper did it, on one knee,
In tones of brute authority.'
That harsher spirit, who before
Had flushed with anger, spoke once more :
'Simple lessons cut most deep.
This lesson in our hearts we keep :

Persuasion, protest, arguments,
The milder forms of violence,
Earn nothing but polite neglect.
England, the way to your respect
Is via murderous force, it seems;
You push us to your own extremes.
You condescend to hear us speak
Only when we slap your cheek.
And yet we lack the last technique :
We rap for order with a gun,
The issues simplify to one
— Then your Democracy insists
You mustn't talk with terrorists !
White and yellow, black and blue,
Have learnt their history from you :
Divide and ruin, muddle through,
Not principled, but politic.
— In strength, perfidious; weak, a trick
To make good men a trifle sick.
We speak in wounds. Behold this mess.
My curse upon your politesse.'
Another ghost stood forth, and wet
Dead lips that had not spoken yet :
'My curse on the cunning and the bland,
On gentlemen who loot a land
They do not care to understand;
Who keep the natives on their paws
With ready lash and rotten laws;
Then if the beasts erupt in rage
Give them a slightly larger cage
And, in scorn and fear combined,
Turn them against their own kind.
The game runs out of room at last,

A people rises from its past,
The going gets unduly tough
And you have (surely . . . ?) had enough.
The time has come to yield your place
With condescending show of grace
— An Empire-builder handing on.
We reap the ruin when you've gone,
All your errors heaped behind you :
Promises that do not bind you,
Hopes in conflict, cramped commissions,
Faiths exploited, and traditions.'
Bloody sputum filled his throat,
He stopped and coughed to clear it out,
And finished, with his eyes a-glow :
'You came, you saw, you conquered . . . So.
You gorged — and it was time to go.
Good riddance. We'd forget — released —
But for the rubbish of your feast,
The slops and scraps that fell to earth
And sprang to arms in dragon birth.
Sashed and bowler-hatted, glum
Apprentices of fife and drum,
High and dry, abandoned guards
Of dismal streets and empty yards,
Drilled at the codeword "True Religion"
To strut and mutter like a pigeon
"Not An Inch — Up The Queen";
Who use their walls like a latrine
For scribbled magic — at their call,
Straight from the nearest music-hall,
Pope and Devil intertwine,
Two cardboard kings appear, and join
In one more battle by the Boyne!

Who could love them? God above. . .
'Yet pity is akin to love,'
The thirteenth corpse beside him said,
Smiling in its bloody head,
'And though there's reason for alarm
In dourness and a lack of charm
Their cursed plight calls out for patience.
They, even they, with other nations
Have a place, if we can find it.
Love our changeling! Guard and mind it.
Doomed from birth, a cursed heir,
Theirs is the hardest lot to bear,
Yet not impossible, I swear,
If England would but clear the air
And brood at home on her disgrace
— Everything to its own place.
Face their walls of dole and fear
And be of reasonable cheer.
Good men every day inherit
Father's foulness with the spirit,
Purge the filth and do not stir it.
Let them out! At least let in
A breath or two of oxygen,
So they may settle down for good
And mix themselves in the common blood.
We all are what we are, and that
Is mongrel pure. What nation's not
Where any stranger hung his hat
And seized a lover where she sat?'
He ceased and faded. Zephyr blew
And all the others faded too.
I stood like a ghost. My fingers strayed
Along the fatal barricade.

The gentle rainfall drifting down
Over Colmcille's town
Could not refresh, only distil
In silent grief from hill to hill.

A SELECTED LIFE

&

VERTICAL MAN

1972   1973

A SELECTED LIFE

I

Galloping Green: May 1962

HE clutched the shallow drum
and crouched forward, thin
as a beast of prey. The shirt
stretched at his waist. He stared
to one side, toward the others,
and struck the skin cruelly
with his nails. Sharp
as the answering arid bark
his head quivered, counting.

2

Coolea: 6 October 1971

A fine drizzle blew
softly across the tattered valley
onto my glasses, and covered
my mourning suit with tiny drops.

A crow scuffled in the hedge
and floated out with a dark groan
into full view. It flapped up the field
and lit on a rock, and scraped its beak.
It croaked : a voice out of the rock
carrying across the slope. Foretell.

Foretell : the Sullane river winding downward
in darker green through the fields
and disappearing behind his house;
cars parking in the lane; a bare yard;
family and friends collecting in the kitchen;
a shelf there, concertinas sprawled in the dust,
the pipes folded on their bag.
The hole waiting in the next valley.
That.

     A rat lay on its side in the wet,
the grey skin washed clean and fleshy,
the little face wrinkled back in hatred,
the back torn open. A pale string
stretched on the gravel. Devil-martyr;
your sad, mad meat. . .
                   I have interrupted
some thing . . . You! Croaking
on your wet stone. Flesh picker.

The drizzle came thick and fast suddenly.
Down in the village the funeral bell began to beat.

                *

And you. Waiting in the dark chapel.
Packed and ready. Upon your hour.
Leaving. . . A few essentials forgotten

— a standard array of dependent beings,
small, smaller, pale, paler, in black;

— sundry musical effects : a piercing
sweet consort of whistles crying,
goosenecked wail and yelp of pipes,
melodeons snoring in sadness,
drum bark, the stricken
harpsichord's soft crash;

— a lurid cabinet : fire's flames
plotting in the dark; hugger mugger
and murder; collapsing back in laughter.
Angry goblets of Ireland's tears,
stuffed with fire, touch. Salut!
Men's guts ignite and whiten in satisfaction;

— a workroom, askew : fumbling at the table
tittering, pools of idea forming.
A contralto fills the room
with Earth's autumnal angst; the pools coalesce.
Here and there in the shallows dim spirits
glide, poissons de la melancolie.
The banks above are smothered in roses;
among their glowing harmonies, bathed in charm,
a cavalier retires in fancy dress,
embracing her loving prize; two baby angels,
each holding a tasseled curtain-corner,
flutter down, clucking and mocking complacently.
Liquids of romance, babbling
on the concrete floor. Let us draw a veil. . .

3

St. Gobnait's Graveyard, Ballyvourney:
that evening

THE gate creaked in the dusk. The trampled grass,
    soaked and still, was disentangling
among the standing stones
after the day's excess.

A flock of crows circled
the church tower, scattered
and dissolved chattering
into the trees.   Fed.

His first buried night
drew on.   Unshuddering.
And welcome . . .
Shudder for him,

Pierrot limping forward in the sun
out of Merrion Square, long ago,
in black overcoat and beret,
pale as death from his soiled bed,

swallowed back : animus
brewed in clay, uttered
in brief meat and brains, flattened
back under our flowers.

Gold and still he lay,
on his secondlast bed. *Dottore!* A withered smile,
the wry hands lifted. *A little while
and you may not. . .*

[26]

Salut.
Slán.
Yob tvoyu mat'.
Master, your health.

VERTICAL MAN

4

Philadelphia: 3 October 1972

I was pouring a drink when the night-monotony
was startled below by a sudden howling
of engines along Market Street,
curséd ambulances intermixing their screams
down the dark canyons.

Over the gramophone your death-mask
was suddenly awake
and I felt something of you
out in the night, near and moving nearer,
tittering, uneasy.

I thought we had laid you to rest
— that you had been directed toward
crumbling silence, and the like.
It seems it is hard to keep
a vertical man down.

I lifted the glass, and the furies
redoubled their distant screams.
To you : the bourbon-breath.
To me, for the time being,
the real thing. . .

'THERE has grown lately upon the soul
      a covering as of earth and stone,
thick and rough . . .'
                    I had been remembering
the sour ancient phrases . . .
                        'Very well,
seemingly the argument requires it :
let us assume mankind is worth considering . . .'

That particular heaviness.

                        That the days pass,
that our tasks arise, dominate our energies,
are mastered with difficulty and some pleasure,
and are obsolete. That there can be a sweet stir
hurrying in the veins (earned : this sunlight
— this oxygen — are my *reward* !) and the ground
grows dull to the tread. The ugly rack : let it ride.
That you may startle the heart of a whole people
(as you know) and all your power,
with its delicate, self-mocking adjustments,
is soon beating to a coarse pulse
to glut fantasy and sentiment.
That for all you have done, the next beginning
is as lonely, as random, as gauche and unready,
as presumptuous, as the first,
when you stripped and advanced timidly
toward nothing in particular.
Though with a difference — there is
a kind of residue. Not an increase in weight
(we must not become portly; your admired D******,
the lush intellectual glamour loosening
to reveal the travelogue beneath).

But a residue in the timidity,
a maturer unsureness, as we
prepare to undergo preparatory error.

ONLY this morning . . . that desultory moment or two
standing at the rain-stained glass; a while more
looking over the charts pinned on the wall;
to sit down with the folder of notes on the left
and clean paper on the right, the pen beside it,
and remove and put down the spectacles and bury
my face in my hands, in self-devouring prayer,
till the charts and notes come crawling to life again
under a Night seething with
soft incandescent bombardment!

At the dark zenith a pulse beat,
a sperm of light separated wriggling
and snaked in a slow beam down
the curve of the sky, through faint
structures and hierarchies
of elements and things and beasts. It fell,
a packed star, dividing
and redividing until it was
a multiple gold tear. It dropped
toward the horizon, entered
bright Quincunx newly risen,
beat with a blinding flame and dis-
appeared. I stared, duly blinded.
An image burned on the brain
— a woman-animal : scaled,
pierced in paws and heart,
ecstatically calm. It faded
to a far-off desolate call,

                    a child's . . .

If the eye could follow that, accustomed to
that dark . . .
                    But that is your domain.

AT which thought, your presence
    turned back toward the night.
                            (*Wohin* . . .)
                                        Stay
a while. Since you are here.
                        At least
we have *Das Lied von der Erde*
and a decent record-player together
at the one place and time.
                        With a contraction
of the flesh . . . A year exactly since you died !

I arrested the needle. The room filled
with a great sigh. In terror and memory
I lowered the tiny point toward our youth
— into those bright cascades !
                        Radiant outcry —
trumpets and drenching strings — exultant tenor —
Schadenfreude! The waste !
                        Abject. Irrecoverable . . .

                    *

THE golden bourbon winks in the glass. For the road.
    But wait, there is something I must show you first,
a song of cark and care. A drinking — a *drunken* — song
for the misery of this world. . . Not quite right yet
— but very soulful. To give you a hollow laugh.

                    [31]

Let Gloom gather, and deject
   the soul's gardens.
Let Joy shrivel up and die
   and song with it.
For Life is a black business.
   While as for Death —

Therefore, a little music, a little something
   — a timely tumbler.
Earth has not anything
   to show more fair,
Life being what it is.
   And as for Death —

The azure firmament
   is permanent.
The Earth is here to stay
   and always good
for another Primavera.
   Whereas Man —

Would you care to share a queer vision I had?
By your gravestone. . .
                         It was moonlight.
And there was something crouching there —
   ape-shaped ! —
demented, howling out
silent foulness, accursèd silent screams
into the fragrant Night . . .

THE golden goodness trembles. It is time.
And more than time. Kindly
step forward.
                    A black
bloody business,
                    the whole thing . . .

He stepped forward through the cigarette-smoke
to his place at the piano
— all irritation — and tore
off his long fingernails to play.

From palatal darkness a voice
rose flickering, and checked
in glottal silence. The song
articulated and pierced.

We leaned over the shallows from the boat slip
and netted the little grey shrimp-ghosts
snapping, and dropped them
in the crawling biscuit-tin.

THE GOOD FIGHT
A POEM FOR THE TENTH ANNIVERSARY
OF THE DEATH OF
JOHN F. KENNEDY

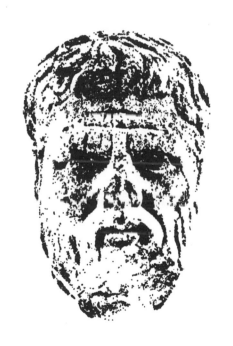

1973

In 1962 . . . people began seriously to calculate that, if the three brothers took the Presidency in succession, it would carry the country to 1984 . . . the succession could then pass to the sons.

> Henry Fairlie, *The Kennedy Promise*, London, 1973.

Those who are imprisoned in the silence of reality always use a gun (or, if they are more fortunate, a pen) to speak for them.

> John Clellon Holmes, 'The Silence of Oswald', *Playboy*, November 1965.

No sir, I killed nobody.

> Lee Harvey Oswald, Dallas Police Headquarters, 22 November 1963.

THE GOOD FIGHT

I

ONCE upon a time a certain phantom
      took to certain red-smelling corridors
in sore need. It met, with a flush of pleasure,
the smell of seed and swallowed
life and doom in the same animal action.

(Mere substance — our metier.
This is our nature, the human mouth
tasting Justice or a favourite soup
with equal relish.)

                    He wiped his lips
and leaned tiredly against the window,
flying through the night. The darkened cabin
creaked under a few weak blue lights.
Outside, half seen, the fields of stars
chilled his forehead, their millions centred on
the navigator.
                    Not commanding. Steering.

Can we believe it possible for anyone
to master the art of steering while he must
at the same time expend his best skill
gaining control of the helm?

                              His hands flexed.
All reasonable things are possible.

All that day, the reporters in the corridor
had pushed closer to the room.
As the hours passed, the press of human beings
— the sweat and smoke — built up
a meaty odour.

Once, he rolled up his sleeve
and looked at the calloused, scratched arm :
'Ohio did that to me.'
(One day in Philadelphia
his hand *burst* with blood.)

He rolled the sleeve down again
and shook his head, not understanding,
then became cool again as ever,
asking : 'Who made that decision?
Who had command decision then?'

*

Shock-headed, light-footed, he swung
an invisible cloak about him in the uproar
and hunched down from the platform at them,
his hands in his jacket pockets.
A jugular pleasure beat in his throat.

'Ever free and strong
we will march along, going to meet
the harsh bright demands of the West, building
a new City on a New Frontier,
where led and leader bend their wills together
in necessary rule — admit
no limit but the possible, grant

[38]

to each endeavour its appointed post,
its opportunity to serve :
our Youth carrying its ideals
into the fettered places of the earth;
our Strength on guard at every door of freedom
around the world; our Art and Music
down from the dark garret — into the sun !
The eyes of the world upon us !'

He held out his inflamed right hand
for the Jaw to grip. The sinews winced.
Crude hand-lettered signs danced in the murk.

'Forward, then, in higher urgency,
adventuring with risk,
raising each other to our moral best,
aspiring to the sublime
in warlike simplicity, our power
justified upon our excellence !

If other nations falter
their people still remain what they were.
But if our country in its call to greatness
falters, we are little but the scum
of other lands. That is our special danger,
our burden and our glory.
The accident that brought our people together
out of blind necessities
— embrace it ! — explosive — to our bodies.'

(It sounds as though it could go on for ever,
yet there is a shape to it — Appropriate
Performance. Another almost perfect
working model. . . But it gets harder.
The concepts jerk and wrestle, back to back.

The finer the idea the harder it is
to assemble lifelike. It adopts hardnesses
and inflexibilities, knots, impossible joints
made possible only by stress,
and good for very little afterward.)

'Welcome challenge, that can stretch
the two sinews of the Soul,
Body and Mind, to a pure pitch,
so we may strike the just note
inside and out. . .'

                        'Peace — a process,
a way of solving problems. . .'
                                        'Leisure —
an opportunity to perfect
those things of which we now despair. . .'

' — Let us make ourselves vessels of decision !
We are not here to curse the darkness.
The old order changes ! Men
firm in purpose and clear in thought
channel by their own decisions
forces greater than any man !'

The swaying mass exclaimed
about the great
dream
            steps. . .

(Where is a young man's heart in such a scene?
Who would not be stunned by the beast's opinion?
Nor think wisdom control of the beast's moods?

[40]

What schooling will resist, and not be swamped
and swept downstream? What can a young man do?
Especially if he belong to a great city
and be one of her rich and noble citizens
and also fine to look upon, and tall?)

He turned to go, murmuring aside
with a boyish grin :
                    'If anybody calls
say I am
raping the intellectuals !'

Inside, a group of specialists,
chosen for their incomparable dash,
were gathered around
a map of the world's regions
with all kinds of precision instruments.

II

A lonely room.
              An electric fire
glowing in one corner. He is lying on his side.
It is late. He is at the centre of a city,
awake.

        Above and below him
there are other rooms, with others in them.
He knows nobody as yet, and has
no wish to. Outside the window
the street noises ascend.

His cell hangs in the night.

He could give up.
But there is something he must do.

And though the night passes, and the morning
brings back familiarity, and he goes out
about his business as though nothing had changed
— energyless at his assigned tasks —
and though the evening comes and he discovers
for the first time where to buy bread and tomatoes,
milk and meat, and climbs the dirty stairs
and takes possession for the second time,
and soon discovers how to light the gas
and where to put things, and where to sit
so he can read and eat at the same time,
and reads a long time
with the crumbs hardening and a tawny scum
shrinking on the cold tea, and finally
ventures out for his first night prowl
and takes possession of his neighbourhood,
learning at each turn, and turns for home,
and takes possession for the third time,
and reads, and later settles to sleep; and though
next morning he wakes up to a *routine*
for the first time, and goes to work,
repeats his necessary purchases
and manages the routine a little better,
with a less conscious effort; and night begins
to bring familiarity, and finds him
beginning to think at last
of what he is here for; and night follows night
and on a certain evening he puts aside

[42]

his cup and plate, and draws his journal to him
and revolves his pen meditatively. . .

I cannot reach or touch anything.
I cannot lay my hand with normal weight
on anything. It is either nothing
or too much.
                    I have stood out
in the black rain and waited
and concentrated among
those over-lit ruins
irritable and hungry
and not known what city.

I have glided in loveless dream transit
over the shadowy sea floor,
satisfied in the knowledge
that if I once slacken in my savagery
I will drown.

I have watched my own
theatrical eyes narrow
and noted under what stress
and ceaseless changes of mind.
I have seen very few
cut so dull and driven a figure,
masked in scorn or abrupt
impulse, knowing content
nowhere.
                    And I have forgotten
what rain and why I waited
what city from room to room
forgotten what father. . .

                                    But not
what hunger as I move
toward some far sum-total,
attacked under others' eyes.

I have seen myself, a 'thing'
in my own eyes, lifting
my hand empty and opening
and closing my mouth
in senseless mimicry
and wondered why I am alive
or why a man can live in this way.

I believed once that silence
encloses each one of us.
Now, if that silence does not
enclose *each*, as I am led
more and more to understand
— so that I truly am cut off,
a 'thing' in their eyes also —
I can, if my daydreams are right,
decide to end it.

Soak wrist in cold water
to numb the pain.
Then slash my left wrist.
Then plunge wrist into bathtub of hot water.
Somewhere, a violin plays,
as I watch my life whirl away.
I think to myself 'How easy to Die'
and 'A Sweet Death', (to violins).

Or I might reach out and touch.
And he would turn this way
inquiring — Who was that!
What decision was this. . .

	An ambitious man, in a city
and not justice?	where honour is the dominant
	principle, is soon broken upon the
	city as a ship is broken on a
	reef.

Passion, ignorance and concupis-
cence are obscurities clouding
the soul's natural judgment. They
are the origin of crime.

	There is none so small or so high
	but that he shall pay the fitting
	penalty, either in this world or in
yet more savage!	some yet more savage place
conveyed!	whither he shall be conveyed. . .

Great crimes, that sink into the
abyss. . .

Images of evil in a foul
pasture. . .

	— There are those,
	lower still, that seat Greed and
	Money on their throne, and make
squat!	Reason and the Spirit squat on
	the floor under it. . .

[45]

— Democracy cries out for Tyranny; and the Tyrant becomes a wolf instead of a man. . .

The rest! The whole world but one! An impossible logic-being.

— The rest damned to a constant flux of pain and pleasure. They struggle greedily for their pleasures, and butt and kick with horns and hoofs of iron.

man   beast

(d)amn

          best

mean

         r i

team   b a ns
            ^ ^

meat

I wonder what would happen if somebody was to stand up and say he was utterly opposed not only to the government but to the people, to the entire land and complete foundations of his society?

[46]

III

S HE was humming to herself
   among the heavy-scented magnolia bowers,
chic, with shining eyes, smiling at
Power and its attendant graces,
Aphrodite in Washington,

when all of a sudden a black
shadow or a black ruin
or a cliff of black
crossed at rigid speed
and spoiled everything.

Everybody started throwing themselves down
and picking themselves up and running
around the streets looking in each other's face
and saying 'Catastrophe' and weeping
and saying 'Well! That's that.'

For a few days great numbers of people
couldn't sleep, and lost appetite. Children experienced
alarm at the sight of their parents crying.
There were many who admitted
they expected the President's ghost to appear.

Various forms of castration dreads emerged,
probably out of fear of retribution
for unconscious parricidal wishes.
Anxiety was widespread, with apprehension
of worse things to come.

It was unhealthy — a distortion of normal attitudes.
Things had been exalted
altogether out of proportion. Afterward,
when the shock was over, matters settled down
with surprising swiftness, almost with relief :

shudder
and return
                    — a fish, flung back,
that lay stunned, shuddered into consciousness,
and dived back into the depths.

And somewhere in some laughable echo-chamber, for ever,
a prayer came snarling through devilish electrical smoke,
and, blinded by the light reflecting from
the snow everywhere, Dr. Frost tottered forward
scratching his head, and opening his mouth :

IV

I am in disarray. Maybe if I
were to fumble through my papers again. . .
I can no longer, in the face of so much
— so much. . .
                    It is very hard.

I say this that you may know.

But there is nothing for it. On this
everything in me is agreed.

[48]

So, weak a thousand ways,
I have come, I have made toward this place,
among wells of profound energy
and monuments to power and tedium. . .
Not in judgment, and not
in acceptance either.
                              Uncertain.
For if all you wish to do
is curse the world and your place in it
— well then. . .
                    But some appetite
is not satisfied
with that, is dissatisfied unless —

The manipulation, the special pleading,
the cross-weaving of these
'vessels of decision',
the one so 'heroic',
the other so. . .
                    You have to
wear them down against each other
to get any purchase,
and then there is this
strain.
        That all *un*reasonable things
are possible. *Everything*
that can happen will happen. . .

My brothers, huddled in wait,
feeble warriors, self-chosen,
in our secondary world. . .
— who can't take our eyes off anything;
who harp on Love and Art and Truth too often :

[49]

it is appropriate for us
to proceed now and make our attempts
in private, to shuffle off and disappoint
Plato.
      (His 'philosophic nature'
— balance, you will remember;
apportionment, as between Mind and Body!
Harmony, and proper pitch!
The Dance!)

      Plump and faithless;
cut, as it were, in the sinews
of our souls; each other's worst company;
it is we, letting things *be*,
who might come at understanding.
That is the source of our patience.
Reliable first in the direction
and finally in the particulars of our response,
fumbling from doubt to doubt,
one day we might knock
our papers together, and elevate them
(with a certain self-abasement)
— their gleaming razors
mirroring a primary world
where power also is a source of patience
for a while before the just flesh
falls back in black dissolution in its box.

ONE

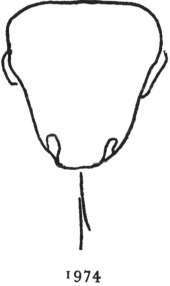

1974

The storyteller's face
turned toward the fire.
He honed his flickering blade.

The sun tunneled onward
eating into the universe's thin dusts
with the World waltzing after it

— Bith, a planetary pearl-blue
flushed with sheets of light,
signed with a thin white wake,

the Voyage of the First Kindred

Up and awake. Up straight
in absolute hunger
out of this black lair, and eat!

Driven rustling blind over
fragments of old frights and furies,
then with a sudden hiss into
a grey sheen of light. A pale space
everywhere alive with bits and pieces,
little hearts beating in their
furryfeathery bundles, transfixed.

That. There.
Hurling toward it, whimswift.
Snapdelicious. So necessary.
Another. Throbflutter. Swallowed.
And another.
The ache. . . The ease!
And another.

But with the satisfaction
comes a falling off
in the drive, the desire.
The two energies approach and come to terms,
balance somehow, grow still.

Afterward I dreamed that I was sprawled out
winding across the heavens.
The first part of my dream was dominated
by thrashing wings, a gaping beak
— some natural threat out of the void.
I associate this, in its origins,
with the difficulties of digestion,

[53]

in its circumstantial detail
with an awareness (not amounting to guilt)
of the many little sufferers involved.

I passed the second and deeper part passively,
supported, captive, in a cosmic grip.
It seemed timeless, but during this period
my body aged, the skin loosened.
I associate this with the process of absorption.

In the third part of the dream I saw
—I was—two discs of light in the heavens
trembling in momentary balance.
They started to part. . . There would be a pang, I knew.
I associate this with the return of hunger.

During the last part I am coiled in combat
with giant particular forces among the stars,
writhing to escape. I manage it
in a final spasm, leaving my decrepit skin
clutched in fierce hands, and plunge downward,
fragments falling after me through space.

Down! Like a young thing!
Coil, now, and wait.
Sleep on these things.

Shortly before the first hour,
at dead of night, a wave of cold
came from below, the Shades stirred
in their noble chairs. The stage before them
lightened and discovered dirt,
a neglected pavement, an ivied corner
with metal gates and temple pillars
— a mean backdrop : a broad street
with boarded windows and scribbled walls.
Down against the temple steps
a metal grating set in the floor
creaked open, emitting first
a puff of some contrived fumes
fitful with theatrical fire,
then a pinkish glitter of chrome.
A tableau rattled up from the crypt :
a man, sporting a striped jacket,
posed in confident quackery, bearded;
a woman, drawn up like a queen,
rouged and spangled. A round pot
bubbled on a stand between them
leaking a phosphorescent mist.
The lift stopped. Something flashed
in his right hand as he reached out
to touch the vessel's rim, once.
Faint strains of music stole
out of the fumes, and filled the air
— the entire fabric sang softly.
He paced forward. A spotlight struck :
he peered in mock intensity,
a hand cupped behind an ear,

[55]

out at the waiting dark, as if
searching the distance. He made to speak.
Above the temple, in the flies,
a mechanism began to whirr.

FINISTERE

I

One . . .

I smelt the weird Atlantic.
Finistère . . .
        Finisterre . . .

The sea surface darkened. The land behind me,
and all its cells and cists, grew dark.
From a bald boulder on the cairn top
I spied out the horizon to the northwest
and sensed that minute imperfection again.
Where the last sunken ray withdrew . . .
A point of light?

A maggot of the possible
wriggled out of the spine
into the brain.

We hesitated before that wider sea
but our heads sang with purpose
and predatory peace.

[56]

And whose excited blood was that
fumbling our movements? Whose ghostly hunger
tunneling our thoughts full of passages
smelling of death and clay and faint metals
and great stones in the darkness?

At no great distance out in the bay
the swell took us into its mercy,
grey upheaving slopes of water
sliding under us, collapsing,
crawling onward, mountainous.

Driven outward a day and a night
we held fast, numbed by the steady
might of the oceanic wind.
We drew close together, as one,
and turned inward, salt chaos
rolling in silence all around us,
and listened to our own mouths
mumbling in the sting of spray :
        — Ill wind end well
        mild mother
        on wild water pour peace

        who gave us our unrest
        whom we meet and unmeet
        in whose yearning shadow
        we erect our great uprights
        and settle fulfilled
        and build and are still
        unsettled, whose goggle gaze
        and holy howl we have scraped
        speechless on slabs of stone

[57]

poolspirals opening on
closing spiralpools
and dances drilled in the rock
in coil zigzag angle and curl
river ripple earth ramp
suncircle moonloop . . .
in whose outflung service
we nourished our hunger
uprooted and came

in whale hell

        gale gullet

salt hole

      dark nowhere

calm queen

       pour peace

The bad dream ended at last.
In the morning, in a sunny breeze,
bare headlands rose fresh out of the waves.
We entered a deep bay, lying open
to all the currents of the ocean.
We were further than anyone had ever been
and light-headed with exhaustion and relief
— three times we misjudged and were nearly driven
on the same rock.
        (I had felt all this before . . .)
We steered in along a wall of mountain
and entered a quiet hall of rock echoing
to the wave-wash and our low voices.
I stood at the prow. We edged to a slope of stone.

[58]

I steadied myself. 'Our Father . . .', someone said
and there was a little laughter. I stood
searching a moment for the right words.
They fell silent. I chose the old words once more
and stepped out. At the solid shock
a dreamy power loosened at the base of my spine
and uncoiled and slid up through the marrow.
A flow of seawater over the rock fell back
with a she-hiss, plucking at my heel.
My tongue stumbled

Who
        is a breath
that makes the wind
that makes the wave
that makes   this   voice?

Who
        is the bull with seven scars
the hawk on the cliff
the salmon sunk in his pool
the pool sunk in her soil
the animal's fury
the flower's fibre
a teardrop in the sun?

Who
        is the word that spoken
the spear springs
        and pours out terror
the spark springs
        and burns in the brain?

[59]

When men meet on the hill
dumb as stones in the dark
        (the craft knocked behind me)
who is the jack of all light?
Who goes in full into
the moon's interesting conditions?
Who fingers the sun's sink hole?
        (I went forward, reaching out)

THE OLDEST PLACE

We approached the shore. Once more.
                        Repeated memory
shifted among the green-necked confused waves.
The sea wind and spray tugged and refreshed us,
but the stale reminder of our sin still clung.

We would need to dislodge
the flesh itself, to dislodge that
— shrivel back to the first drop
and be spat back shivering into
the dark beyond our first father.

                        *

We fished and fowled and chopped at the forest,
cooked and built, ploughed and planted,
danced and drank, all as before.
But worked inland, and got further.

[60]

And there was something in the way the land behaved :
passive, but responding. It grew under our hands.
We worked it like a dough to our requirements
yet it surprised us more than once
with a firm life of its own, as if
it used us.
          Once, as we were burying
one of our children, the half-dug grave
dampened, and overbrimmed, and the water
ran out over the land and would not stop
until the place had become a lake.

                      *

Year followed year.
The first skin blemishes appeared,
and it almost seemed we had been waiting for them.
The sickness and the dying began again.

To make things easier, we decided
to come together in one place.
We thought of the bare plain we found first,
with the standing stone : miles of dead clay
without a trace of a root or a living thing.
We gathered there and the sick died
and we covered them. Others fell sick
and we covered them, fewer and fewer.
A day came when I fell down by the great stone
alone, crying, at the middle of the stinking plain.

                      *

[61]

Night fell, and I lay there face down,
and I dreamed that my ghost stood up
. and faint starry shadows everywhere
lifted themselves up and began
searching about among themselves for something,
hesitant at first, but quickly certain,
and all turning

        — muscular nothingnesses,
demons, animal-heads, wrestling vaguely toward me
reaching out terrible gifts into my face,
clawfuls of dripping cloth
and gold and silver things.
They passed through me. . .

        To the stone,
and draped it with their gifts, murmuring,
and dropped them about its base.
With each gift, the giver
sighed and melted away,
the black stone packed more
with dark radiance.

        And I dreamed
that my ghost moved toward it, hand on heart,
the other hand advanced. . .
        And its glare
gathered like a pulse, and struck
on the withered plain of my own brain.

        *

A draped black shaft under the starlight,
with bars and blocks and coils of restless metal
piled about it, and eyes hovering
above those abnormal stirrings.
A little higher, where there might have been branches,
a complex emptiness shimmered in front of the stars.

A shawl shifted on the top, dangled
black and silver, a crumpled face
with forehead torn crisscross, begging,
with tongue flapping,
and dropped to earth.

38 PHOENIX STREET

Look.
        I was lifted up
past rotten bricks weeds
to look over the wall.
A mammy lifted up a baby on the other side.
Dusty smells. Cat. Flower bells
hanging down purple red.

Look.
        The other. Looking.
My finger picked at a bit of dirt
on top of the wall and a quick
wiry redgolden thing
ran back down a little hole.

                    *

We knelt up on our chairs in the lamplight
and leaned on the brown plush, watching the gramophone.
The turning record shone and hissed
under the needle, liftfalling, liftfalling.
John McCormack chattered in his box.

Two little tongues of flame burned
in the lamp chimney, wavering
their tips. On the glassy belly
little drawnout images quivered.
Jimmy's mammy was drying the delph in the shadows.

                    *

Mister Cummins always hunched down
sad and still beside the stove,
with his face turned away toward the bars.
His mouth so calm, and always set so sadly.
A black rubbery scar stuck on his white forehead.

Sealed in his sad cave. Hisshorror erecting
slowly out of its rock nests, nosing the air.
He was buried for three days under a hill of dead,
the faces congested down all round him
grinning *Dardanelles!* in the dark.

They noticed him by a thread of blood
glistening among the black crusts on his forehead.
His heart gathered all its weakness, to beat.

A worm hanging down, its little round
black mouth open. Sad father.

*

I spent the night there once
in a strange room, tucked in against the wallpaper
on the other side of our own bedroom wall.

Up in a corner of the darkness the Sacred Heart
leaned down in his long clothes over a red oil lamp
with his women's black hair and his eyes lit up in red,
hurt and blaming. He held out the Heart
with his women's fingers, like a toy.

The lamp-wick, with a tiny head
of red fire, wriggled in its pool.
The shadows flickered : the Heart beat !

[65]

MINSTREL

He trailed a zither from
melancholy pale fingers, sighing.
A mist of tears lay still upon the land.

The fire burned down in the grate.
A light burned on the bare ceiling.
A dry teacup stained the oil cloth
where I wrote, bent like a feeding thing
over my own source.

A spoonful of white ash fell
with a soundless puff, undetected.
A shadow, or the chill of night,
advanced out of the corner.
I stopped, my hand lifted
an inch from the page.

Outside, the heavens listened,
a starless diaphragm
stopped miles overhead
to hear the remotest whisper
of returning matter, missing
an enormous black beat.

The earth stretched out in answer.
Little directionless instincts
uncoiled from the wet mud-cracks,
crept in wisps of purpose, and vanished
leaving momentary traces
of claw marks, breasts,
ribs, feathery prints,

[66]

eyes shutting and opening
all over the surface.
A distant point of light
winked at the edge of nothing.

A knock on the window
and everything in fantasy fright
flurried and disappeared.
My father looked in from the dark,
my face black-mirrored beside his.

HIS FATHER'S HANDS

I drank firmly
and set the glass down between us firmly.
You were saying.

My father.
Was saying.

His finger prodded and prodded,
marring his point. Emphas-
emphasemphasis.

I have watched
his father's hands before him

    cupped, and tightening the black Plug
between knife and thumb,
carving off little curlicues
to rub them in the dark of his palms,

[67]

or cutting into new leather at his bench,
levering a groove open with his thumb,
insinuating wet sprigs for the hammer.

He kept the sprigs in mouthfuls
and brought them out in silvery
units between his lips.

I took a pinch out of their hole
and knocked them one by one into the wood,
bright points among hundreds gone black,
other children's — cousins and others, grown up.

    Or his bow hand scarcely moving,
scraping in the dark corner near the fire,
his plump fingers shifting on the strings.

To his deaf, inclined head
he hugged the fiddle's body,
whispering with the tune

with breaking heart
whene'er I hear
in privacy, across a blocked void,

the wind that shakes the barley.
The wind. . .
round her grave. . .

on my breast in blood she died. . .
But blood for blood without remorse
I've ta'en. . .

Beyond that.

*

Your family, Thomas, met with and helped
many of the Croppies in hiding from the Yeos
or on their way home after the defeat
in south Wexford. They sheltered the Laceys
who were later hanged on the Bridge in Ballinglen
between Tinahely and Anacorra.

From hearsay, as far as I can tell
the Men Folk were either Stone Cutters
or masons or probably both.
                              In the 18
and late 1700s even the farmers
had some other trade to make a living.

They lived in Farnese among a Colony
of North of Ireland or Scotch settlers left there
in some of the dispersals or migrations
which occurred in this Area of Wicklow and Wexford
and Carlow. And some years before that time
the Family came from somewhere around Tullow.

Beyond that.

                              *

Littered uplands. Dense grass. Rocks everywhere,
wet underneath, retaining memory of the long cold.

First, a prow of land
chosen, and webbed with tracks;
then boulders chosen
and sloped together, stabilized in menace.

[69]

I do not like this place.
I do not think the people who lived here
were ever happy. It feels evil.
Terrible things happened.
I feel afraid here when I am on my own.

*

Dispersals or migrations.
Through what evolutions or accidents
toward that peace and patience
by the fireside, that blocked gentleness. . .

That serene pause, with the slashing knife,
in kindly mockery,
as I busy myself with my little nails
at the rude block, his bench.

The blood advancing
— gorging vessel after vessel —
and altering in them
one by one.

Behold, that gentleness already
modulated twice, in others :
to earnestness and iteration;
to an offhandedness, repressing various impulses.

*

Extraordinary. . . The big block — I found it
years afterward in a corner of the yard
in sunlight after rain
and stood it up, wet and black :
it turned under my hands, an axis
of light flashing down its length,
and the wood's soft flesh broke open,
countless little nails
squirming and dropping out of it.

The great cell of nightmare rose in pallor
and shed its glare down on the calm gulf.
A woman waited at the edge, with lank hair.
She spread it out. It stiffened and moved
by itself, glistening on her shoulders.

We squirmed in expectation. Then there rose
a suffused heart, stopped, clenched on its light.
'Reap us!' we hissed, in praise. The heart beat
and broke open, and sent a fierce beam
among our wriggling sheaves.

Caught in her cold fist, I writhed and reversed.

*

Mostly the thing runs smoothly, the fall is cradled
immediately in a motherly warmth, with nothing
to disturb the dark urge, except from within
— a tenseness, as it coils on itself, changing
to obscure substance.

Anxieties pass through it,
but it can make no sense of them. It knows
only that it is nightmare-bearing tissue
and that there are others. They drift together
through 'incommunicable' dark, one by one,

toward the dawn zone, not knowing nor caring
that they share anything.
                        Awakening,
their ghost-companionship dissolves back
into private shadow, not often called upon.

[72]

1976

My dear master, I am over forty. I am tired out with tricks and shufflings. I cry from morning till night for rest, rest; and scarcely a day passes when I am not tempted to go and live in obscurity and die in peace in the depths of my old country. There comes a time when all ashes are mingled. Then what will it boot me to have been Voltaire or Diderot, or whether it is your three syllables or my three syllables that survive? One must work, one must be useful, one owes an account of one's gifts, etcetera, etcetera. Be useful to men! Is it quite clear that one does more than amuse them, and that there is much difference between the philosopher and the flute-player? They listen to one and the other with pleasure or disdain, and remain what they were. The Athenians were never wickeder than in the time of Socrates, and perhaps all they owe to his existence is a crime the more. That there is more spleen than good sense in all this, I admit — and back to the Encyclopedia I go.

Diderot to Voltaire, 19 February, 1758
trans. John Viscount Morley

No one did anything at first.
There was no hope.
We were slumped there in the dark, like lead.
Anyone could have done anything with us.

Then someone with backbone made a move
— wherever he found the energy —
and started wriggling away.

After a while another set out across the mud
calling back uneasily for anybody else.
The voice, in a momentary stillness, echoed.
We heard sharp breathing, and then
a body floundering off in the wet.

Then a third.
That decided it for me.
I felt the whole past and future pressing on me,
the millions — even the One! —
that might not live unless. . .
I swore there would be no waste. No waste!

I started. There was one more after me
then the whole world exploded behind us
and a golden light blasted us out.

We found each other afterwards,
inert and stunned, but alive.
Five.

I

Blessed William Skullbullet
glaring from the furnace of your hair
thou whose definitions — whose insane nets —
plunge and convulse to hold thy furious catch
let our gaze blaze, we pray,
let us see how the whole thing
                                                works

II

You will note firstly that there is no containing skin
as we understand it, but 'contained' muscles
— separate entities, interwound and overlaid,
firm, as if made of fish-meat or some
stretched blend of fibre and fat.
This one, for example, containing — functioning as —
a shoulderblade; or this one like a strap
reaching underneath it, its tail
melting into a lower rib; or this one
nuzzling into the crease of the groin;
or this, on the upper arm, like a big leech;
even the eyes — dry staring buttons of muscle.
It would seem possible to peel the body asunder,
to pick off the muscles and let them
drop away one by one writhing
until you had laid bare
four or five simple bones at most.
Except that at the first violation
the body would rip into pieces and fly apart
with terrible spasms.

[77]

A figure struck and lodged in the earth
  and squatted, buried to the knees.
It stared, absolutely tense.
  Time passed.

It settled gradually
  working like a root into the soil.
After it was fixed firmly
  the pent energy released inward.

Clarity and lightness
  opened in the hollow of the head.
Articulation, *capacity*,
  itched in the thumbs and fingers.

The heart fibres loosened as they dried
  and tangled back among themselves.
The whole interior of the body
  became an empty dry space.

The stare faded in the eyes
  which grew watchful, then passive
— lenses, letting the light pass easily
  in either direction.

The face went solid
  and set in a thick mask
on jaws and neck.
  The lips adhered.

The brow went blank.
   Hands and fingers found each other
and joined on his lap.
   He grew weightless,

the solid posture
   grew graceful.
A light architecture.
   No-stress against no-stress.

The seam of the lips
   widened minutely in a smile.
The outer corners of the eyes crinkled.
   The lenses grew opaque, and began to glow.

And so he departed, leaving a mere shell
   — that serene effigy
we have copied so much
   and set everywhere :

on mountaintops, at the sources of streams,
   hid in caves, sunk in the depths of the sea,
perched on pillars in the desert,
   fixed in tree forks,

on car bonnets, on the prows
   of ships and trains,
stood on shelves, in fanlights,
   over stable doors, planted under foundation stones,

attached to our women
   in miniature : on their ears
or at their wrists, or disappearing on pendants
   down their dark bosoms.

[79]

IV

The point, greatly enlarged,
pushed against the skin
depressing an area of tissue.
Rupture occurred : at first a separation
at the intensest place among the cells
then a deepening damage
with nerve-strings fraying
and snapping and writhing back.
Blood welled up to fill the wound,
bathing the point as it went deeper.

Persist.
   Beyond a certain depth
it stands upright by itself
and quivers with borrowed life.

Persist.
   And you may find
the buried well. And take on
the stillness of a root.

Quietus.

   Or :

V

A blade licks out and acts
with one tongue.
Jets of blood respond
in diverse tongues.

And promptly.
A single sufficient cut
and the body drops at once.
No reserve. Inert.

If you would care to enter this grove of beasts :

VI

A veteran smiled and let us pass through
to the dripping groves in Swift's slaughterhouse,
hot confusion and the scream-rasp of the saw.
Huge horned fruit not quite dead
— chained, hooked by one hock, stunned
above a pool of steaming spiceblood.

Two elderly men in aprons waded back and forth
with long knives they sharpened slowly and
inserted, tapping cascades of black blood
that collapsed before their faces onto the concrete.
Another fallen beast landed, kicking,
and was hooked by the ankle and hoisted into its place.

They come in behind a plank barrier on an upper level
walking with erect tail to the stunning place. . .
Later in the process they encounter
a man who loosens the skin around their tails
with deep cuts in unexpected directions;
the tail springs back; the hide pulls down to the jaws.

With the sheep it was even clearer
they were dangling alive, the blood trickling
over nostrils and teeth. A flock of them waited their turn

[81]

crowded into the furthest corner of the pen,
some looking back over their shoulders
at us, in our window.

Great bulks of pigs hung from dainty heels,
the full sow-throats cut open the wrong way.
Three negroes stood on a raised bench before them.
One knifed the belly open upward to the tail
until the knife and his hands disappeared
in the fleshy vulva and broke some bone.

The next opened it downward to the throat,
embraced the mass of entrails, lifted them out
and dropped them in a chute. And so to one
who excavated the skull through flaps of the face,
hooked it onto the carcase and pushed all forward
toward a frame of blue flames, the singeing machine.

At a certain point it is all merely meat,
sections hung or stacked in a certain order.
Downstairs a row of steel barrows
holds the liquid heaps of organs.
As each new piece drops, adding itself,
the contents tremble throughout their mass.

In a clean room a white-coated worker
positioned a ham, found a blood vessel with a forceps,
clipped it to a tube of red chemical
and pumped the piece full. It swelled immediately
and saturated : tiny crimson jets
poured from it everywhere. Transfused !

VII

Vital spatterings. Excess.
Make the mind creep. Play-blood
bursting everywhere out of
big chopped dolls : the stuff breaking copiously
out of a slow, horrified head.

Is it all right to do this?
Is it an offence against justice
when someone stumbles away helplessly
and has to sit down
until her sobbing stops?

VIII

How to put it . . . without offence
— even though it is an offence,
monstrous, in itself.

A living thing swallowing another.

Lizards :
            Stone still
holding it sideways in its jaws.
With a jerk, adjusting it
with the head facing nearer.

The two staring in separate directions.

Again. The head inside the mouth
and the little hands and feet and the tail
and the suddenly soft round belly
hanging down outside.

[83]

                              Again.
        Splayed hind legs and a tail.

        A tail.
                Then
        a leather-granite face
        unfulfillable.

                        IX

        A dark hall. Great green liquid windows
        lit. The Stations of the Depths.

        In its deep tank, a leopard shark patrolled
        away from the window, enlarging to a shadow.
        It circled back, grew brighter, reduced
        into blunt focus — a pink down-laugh, white needles —
        and darkened away again, lengthening.

        A herring-flock pelted in spinning water
        staring in place — they trembled with speed
        and fled, shifted and corrected,
        strung together invisibly in their cluster.

        Two morays craned up their exposed shoulders
        from a cleft, the bird-beaked heads
        peering up at a far off music of slaughter,
        moving with it, thick and stiff.

        A still tank. Gross anemones flowered open
        flesh-brilliant on slopes of rock.
        A crayfish, crusted with black detail, dreamed
        on twig tips across the bottom sand.
        A crab fumbled at the lip of a coral shelf
        and a gentle fish cruised outward, and down.

                        [84]

X

It is so peaceful at last :
sinking onward into a free reverie
— if you weren't continually nudged awake
by little scratching sounds
and brushing sounds outside the door
or muffled voices upstairs.

The idea was to be able to step out
into a clean brightness onto a landing
flooded with sun and blowing gauze
like a cool drunkenness, with every speck of dust
filtered out of the air!
To follow the graceful curve of handrail
and relish the new firmness underfoot,
the very joists giving off confidence.

What an expanse of neglect
stretched before us!
Strip to the singlet and prepare,
fix the work with a steady eye,
begin : scraping and scraping
down to the wood,
making it good, treating it. . .
Growing unmethodical after a while,
letting the thing stain and stay unfinished.

And we are going to have to do something
about the garden. All that sour soil
stuffed with mongrel growth
— hinges and bits of slate,
gaspipes plugged with dirt.

Disturb anything and there is
a scurrying of wireworms and ribbed woodlice
or a big worm palely deciding.

That door banging again.
If there is anything I can't stand. . .

We have to dig down;
sieve, scour and roughen;
make it all fertile and vigorous
— get the fresh rain down!

XI

The shower is over.
And there's the sun out again
and the sound of water outside
trickling clean into the shore.
And the little washed bird-chirps and trills.

I have been opening my mind to some new poems
by a neglected 'colleague' of mine
— with some relief. One or two
of a certain quality.

A watered peace. Drop. At the heart.
Drop. The unlikely heart.

A shadow an instant
on the window. A bird.
And the sun is gone in again.

(Good withdrawn, that other good may come.)

[86]

We have shaped and polished.
We have put a little darkness behind us,
we are out of that soup.
Into a little brightness.
That soup.

The mind flexes.
The heart encloses.

XII

It might be just as well not to worry too much
about our other friend.

He was mainly captious and fanciful.
Gifted, certainly, but finally he leaves
a shrug of disappointment.
Good company from time to time
but it was best kept offhand.
Any regularity, any intimacy,
and the veneer. . .
                    Mean as a cat,
always edging for the small advantage.

But he *could* compete.
There isn't a day passes but I thank God
some others I know — I can see them, mounting up
with grim pleasure to the judgment seat —
didn't 'fulfil their promise'.

An arrogant beginning, *then*
the hard attrition.

[87]

Stomach that
and you find a kind of strength not to be had
any other way. Enforced humility,
with all the faculties. Making for
a small excellence — very valuable.

There, at the unrewarding outer reaches,
the integrity of the whole thing is tested.

XIII

Hand lifted. Song.
                    I hear.
Hand on breast. Dear heart.
                              I know.
Hand at the throat. Funnelled blood.
                                        It is yours.
Hand over eyes. I see.
                    I see.

XIV

My eye hurt. I lay down
and pressed it shut into
the palm of my hand.

I slept uneasily
        a dish of ripe eyes gaped up
        at the groaning iron press descending
                and dreamed
I pulled a sheet of brilliant colour
free from the dark.

[88]

XV

The pen writhed. It moved
under my thumb!
        It has sensed
that sad prowler on our landing again.

If she dares come nearer, if she dares. . .
She and her 'sudden and
peremptory incursions'. . .
I'll pierce her like
a soft fruit, a soft big seed!

XVI

The penetrating senses, the intimacy,
the detailed warmth, the touch under the shirt,
all these things, they cling, they delight,
they hold us back. It is a question of
getting separated from one's habits
and stumbling onto another way. The beginning
must be inward. Turn inward. Divide.

A few times in a lifetime, with luck,
the actual *substance* alters : fills with
expectation, beats with a molten glow
as change occurs; grows cool; resumes.

There is a pause at the full
without currents or wind. The shorescape
holds its thousand mirrors and waits.
Weed rustles in a cleft
and it is not the wind. In a nearby pool
elements of memory are stalking one another.

[89]

XVII

A smell of hot home-made loaves
came from the kitchen downstairs.

A sheet of yellowish Victorian thick paper,
a few spearheads depicted in crusty brown ink
— Viking remains at Islandbridge —
added their shiny-stale smell to the baked air
like dried meat.

              Man-meat, spitted.
Corpses scattered on the river mud
in suds of blood, a few here and there
with broken-off spears buried in them,
buried with them, preserving the points
unweathered for a period.
                    For, let me see . . .
a few years — say a lifetime —
(That bread smells delicious !)
over the even thousand years.

XVIII

Asia : great deserts of grass
with poppies and distant cities trembling
in the golden wind. Whole centuries
(if I have it even partly right)
valuing passive watchfulness — not to fuss.

Ah well. . .
              Grind it up, wash it down,
stoke the blind muscular furnace,
keep the waste volatile
— sieve it : scoop and shake, shiver and tilt.

[90]

Reach up expertly in your shiny boots,
tinker and trim, empty your oil-can
into the hissing navels, tap the flickering dials,
study the massive shimmering accurate flywheels.

It isn't the kind of job you can do properly
without a proper lunch : fresh bread,
ham, a piece of cheese,
an apple, a flask of coffee.
                              Enjoy it
on your deafening bench. . .

                              Outlandish
the things that will come into your mind.
Often you will find yourself standing up
snapping your fingers suddenly
and there's a thing for you !
And you give a skip up the shop-floor.

XIX

It is hard to beat a good meal
and a turn on the terrace,
or a picnic on the beach at evening,
watching the breakers blur and gleam
as the brain skews softly.
Or an enjoyable rest, with a whodunit
under a flowering chestnut, an essay or two
on a park bench, a romance devoured
at one stroke on a grassy slope.

But for real pleasure there is nothing to equal
sitting down to a *serious* read,
getting settled down comfortably for the night
with a demanding book on your knee
and your head intent over it,
eyes bridging the gap, closing a circuit.

Except that it is not a closed circuit,
more a mingling of lives, worlds simmering
in the entranced interval : all that you are
and have come to be
— or as much as can be brought to bear —
'putting on' the fixed outcome of another's
encounter with what what he was
and had come to be
impelled him to stop in flux, living,
and hold that encounter out from
the streaming away of lifeblood, timeblood,
a nexus a nexus
wriggling with life not of our kind.

Until one day as I was . . .

I met a fair maid all shining
with hair all over her cheeks
and pearly tongue
who spoke to me and sighed
as if my own nervous nakedness
spoke to me and said :

My heart is a black fruit.
It is a piece of black coal.
When I laugh a black thing hovers.

XX

Loneliness. An odour of soap.
To this end must we come,
deafened with spent energy.

And so the years propel themselves onward
toward that tunnel, and the stink of fear.

— We can amend that. (Time permits
a certain latitude. Not much,
but a harmless re-beginning :)

'And so the years propel themselves
onward on thickening scars, toward
new efforts of propulsion. . .

XXI

The residue of a person's work. . .

The words 'water' or 'root'
offered in real refreshment. The words
'Love', 'Truth', etc., offered with force
but self-serving, therefore ineffective.
A fading pose — the lonely prowl of the outcast.

Or half a dozen outward howls of glory
and noble despair. Borrowed glory,
his own despair. For the rest, energy wasted
grimacing facetiously inward. And yet
a vivid and lasting image : the racked outcast.

[93]

Or opinion modified or sharpened, in search.
Emotion expelled, to free the structure of a thing,
or indulged, to free the structure of an idea.
The entirety of one's being
crowded for everlasting shelter
into the memory of one crust of bread.
Granting it everlasting life.
Eating it absolutely.

Somehow it all matters ever after — very much —
though each little thing matters little
however painful that may be.

And remember that foolishness
though it may give access to heights of vision
in certain gifted abnormal brains
remains always what it is.

XXII

Where is everybody?
                    Look
in the mirror, at that face.

It began to separate, the head opening
like a rubbery fan. . .
The thin hair blurred and crept apart
widening from a deepening seam
as the forehead opened down the centre
and unfolded pale new detail
surfacing from within.

[94]

The eyes moved wider apart
and another eye surfaced between them and divided.
The nose divided and doubled and moved out
one to right and left.
The mouth stretched in a snarl
then split into two mouths, pursed.

Two faces now returned my stare
each whole yet neither quite 'itself'.
(But then the original could not
have been called 'itself' either.
What but some uneasiness made it divide?)

At any rate my stare now began
to grow unfixed, wandering
from one image to the other
as if losing conviction.

Another ounce of impulse and
I might have driven my fist at the mirror
and abolished everything.
But the starred ruins
would only have started to divide and creep.

XXIII

That day when I woke
a great private blade
was planted in me from bowels to brain.
I lay there alive round it. When I moved
it moved with me, and there was no hurt.
I knew it was not going to go away.
I got up carefully, transfixed.

[95]

From that day forth I knew
what it was to taste reality
and not to; to suffer tedium or pain
and not to; to eat, swallowing with pleasure,
and not to; to yield and fail,
to note this or that withering in me,
and not to; to anticipate
the Breath, the Bite, with cowering arms,
and not to. . .

(Tiny delicate dawn-antelope that go without water
getting all they need in vegetation and the dew.
Night-staring jerboa.
The snapping of their slender bones,
rosy flesh bursting in small sweet screams
against the palate fine. Just a quick
note. Lest we forget.)

Meanwhile, with enormous care,
to the split id — delicate
as a flintflake — the knifed nous. . .

XXIV

It is time I continued my fall.

The divider waits, shaped
razor sharp to my dream print.

I should feel nothing.

Turning slowly and more slowly
we drifted to rest in a warmth of flesh,
twinned, glaring and growing.

[96]

SONG OF THE NIGHT
AND OTHER POEMS

1978

He carried me out of the lamplight.
I hugged his night-smelling overcoat
and let myself loosen with his steps
and my sight swim.
                          Sticks in a black hedge
went flickering past. Frosty twinkles
danced along in the granite.

The light on the next lamp-post
stepped nearer, blue-white, gas-cold.
Nearer, and the living mantle
licked and hummed in its heart.
A stern moon-stare shed all over my brain
as he carried me, warm and chill,
homeward, abandoned, onward to the next shadow.

C. G. JUNG'S 'FIRST YEARS'

I

Dark waters churn amongst us
and whiten against troublesome obstacles :

A nurse's intimate warm ear
far in the past; the sallow loin of her throat;
and more — her song at twilight
as she dreamily (let us now suppose)
combined in her entrails
memories of womanly manipulations
with further detailed plans for the living flesh.

II

Jesus, and his graves eating the dead. . .
A Jesuit — a witchbat —
toiled with outspread sleeves down
the path from a wooded hilltop. . .
A pillar of skin
stared up dumb, enthroned
in an underground room. . .

The dreams broke in succession and ran back
whispering with disappearing particulars.

*

Since when I have eaten Jesus . . .
and stepped onto the path
    long ago : my fingers stretched at the hill
    and a sleeve-winged terror
    shrank like a shadow and flapped away

[99]

sailing over the dry grass;
staring crumbs led up through the tree-darkness
to a hollow, with bloody steps down . . .
and have assumed the throne.

ANNIVERSARIES

1955

He took her, trembling
with decision, into a cage
of flowering arches full of light
to the altar.

They squeezed hands
and waited in happiness.
They were creatures to catch
Nature's attention.

(The three qualities that are necessary
She has, namely : patience,
deliberation,
and skill with the instruments.)

*

And very soon
we were moving outward
together, a fraction
apart.

We preened and shivered
among pale stems
under nodding grain. Breezes nibbled
and fingered at our fur.

We advanced with care.
Sunlight passed direct
into our blood.
Mercury

glittered
in the needle-nails we
sank into the tissuey stems
as we climbed

eyeing each other,
on whom
Nature had as yet
worked so little.

1956

Fifteen minutes or thereabouts
of Prelude and Liebestod
— elephant into orgasm —
and I was about ready.

I crooked my foot
around the chair-leg
and my fingers around
the pen, and set

the star-dome
creaking with music
at absolute zero
across the bankrupt night.

A couple of hundred yards around the corner
in a moon-flooded office in Merrion Street
my Finance files dreamed,
propped at the ledge,

my desk moved
                    infinitesimally.
Over the entire country,
over market and harbour, in silvery light,

emanations of government
materialised and embraced
downward and began
metaphysically to bite.

A small herd of friends
stared back from the Mailboat rail.
A mongrel dog lapped
in a deserted town square.

A book came
fluttering out of the dark
and flapped
at the window.

1975

'Below us in the distance
we came upon
a wide wheatfield breathing
dust-gold.

We flew down
and our claws curled, as one,
around the same outer branch
steadily, as it shook.

Our eyes thrilled
together : loaded
stems dipped everywhere
under mouse-fruit. . .'

1975
an alternative

'Once in the long flight we swerved low,
supported on each other's presences.
Our shadows raced flickering over stubble
sprinkled with eyepoints of fierce fright and malice.

The urge to strangle at them with our feet!

Then re-ascended. . .'

A species of wide range,
they feed generally at height,
the more enduring as they grow tireder;
starving if needs be; living on their own waste.

ARTISTS' LETTERS

Folders, papers, proofs, maps
with tissue paper marked and coloured.
I was looking for something,
confirmation of something,
in the cardboard box
when my fingers deflected among
fat packets of love letters,
old immediacies in elastic bands.

I shook a letter open from
its creases, carefully, and read
— and shrugged, embarrassed.
                              Then stirred.
My hand grew thin and agitated
as the words crawled again
quickly over the dried paper.

Letter by letter the foolishness
deepened, but displayed
a courage in its own unsureness;
acknowledged futility and waste
in all their importance . . . a young idiocy
in desperate full-hearted abandon
to all the chance of one choice :

There is one throw, no more. One
offering : make it. With no style
— these are desperate times. There is
a poverty of spirit in the wind,
a shabby richness in braving it.
My apologies, but you are my beloved
and I will not be put off.

What is it about such letters,
torn free ignominiously
in love? Character stripped off
our pens plunge repeatedly
at the unique cliché, cover
ache after ache of radiant paper
with analytic ecstasies,
wrestle in repetitious fury.

The flesh storms our brain; we storm
our entranced opposite, badger her
with body metaphors, project
our selves with outthrust stuttering arms,
cajoling, forcing her
— her spread-eagled spirit —
to accept our suspect cries
with shocked and shining eyes.

Artists' letters (as the young career
grows firmer in excited pride
and moves toward authority
after the first facetiousness,
the spirit shaken into strength
by shock after shock of understanding)
suddenly shudder and *display*! Animal.
Violent vital organs of desire.

A toothless mouth opens
and we throw ourselves, enthralled, against our bonds
and thrash toward her. And when we have
been nicely eaten and our parts
spat out whole and have become
'one', *then* we can settle our cuffs
and our Germanic collar
and turn back calmly toward distinguished things.

TAO AND UNFITNESS
AT INISTIOGUE ON THE RIVER NORE

Noon

The black flies kept nagging in the heat.
Swarms of them, at every step, snarled
off pats of cow dung spattered in the grass.

Move, if you move, like water.

The punts were knocking by the boathouse, at full tide.
Volumes of water turned the river curve
hushed under an insect haze.

                              Slips of white,
trout bellies, flicked in the corner of the eye
and dropped back onto the deep mirror.

Respond. Do not interfere. Echo.

Thick green woods along the opposite bank
climbed up from a root-dark recess
eaved with mud-whitened leaves.

                     *

In a matter of hours all that water is gone,
except for a channel near the far side.
Muck and shingle and pools where the children
wade, stabbing flatfish.

Afternoon

Inistiogue itself is perfectly lovely,
like a typical English village, but a bit sullen.
Our voices echoed in sunny corners
among the old houses; we admired
the stonework and gateways, the interplay
of roofs and angled streets.

The square, with its 'village green', lay empty.
The little shops had hardly anything.
The Protestant church was guarded by a woman
of about forty, a retainer, spastic
and indistinct, who drove us out.

An obelisk to the Brownsfoords and a Victorian
Celto-Gothic drinking fountain, erected
by a Tighe widow for the villagers,
'erected' in the centre. An astronomical-looking
sundial stood sentry on a platform
on the corner where High Street went up out of the square.

We drove up, past a long-handled water pump
placed at the turn, with an eye to the effect,
then out of the town for a quarter of a mile
above the valley, and came to the dead gate
of Woodstock, once home of the Tighes.

*

The great ruin presented its flat front
at us, sunstruck. The children disappeared.
Eleanor picked her way around a big fallen branch

and away along the face toward the outbuildings.
I took the grassy front steps and was gathered up
in a brick-red stillness. A rook clattered out of the dining room.

A sapling, hooked thirty feet up
in a cracked corner, held out a ghost-green
cirrus of leaves. Cavities
of collapsed fireplaces connected silently
about the walls. Deserted spaces, complicated
by door-openings everywhere.

There was a path up among bushes and nettles
over the beaten debris, then a drop, where bricks
and plaster and rafters had fallen into the kitchens.
A line of small choked arches. . . The pantries, possibly.

Be still, as though pure.

A brick, and its dust, fell.

Nightfall

The trees we drove under in the dusk
as we threaded back along the river through the woods
were no mere dark growth, but a flitting-place
for ragged feeling, old angers and rumours. . .

Black and Tan ghosts up there, at home
on the Woodstock heights : an iron mouth
scanning the Kilkenny road : the house
gutted by the townspeople and burned to ruins. . .

The little Ford we met, and inched past, full of men
we had noticed along the river bank during the week,
disappeared behind us into a fifty-year-old night.
Even their caps and raincoats. . .

Sons, or grandsons. Poachers.
                              Mud-tasted salmon
slithering in a plastic bag around the boot,
bloodied muscles, disputed since King John.

The ghosts of daughters of the family
waited in the uncut grass as we drove
down to our mock-Austrian lodge and stopped.

*

We untied the punt in the half-light, and pushed out
to take a last hour on the river, until night.
We drifted, but stayed almost still.
The current underneath us
and the tide coming back to the full
cancelled in a gleaming calm, punctuated
by the plop of fish.

Down on the water. . . at eye level. . . in the little light
remaining overhead. . . the mayfly passed in a loose drift,
thick and frail, a hatch slow with sex,
separate morsels trailing their slack filaments,
olive, pale evening dun, imagoes, unseen eggs
dropping from the air, subimagoes, the river filled
with their nymphs ascending and excited trout.

Be subtle, as though not there.

[110]

We were near the island — no more than a dark mass
on a sheet of silver — when a man appeared in midriver
quickly and with scarcely a sound, his paddle touching
left and right of the prow, with a sack behind him.
The flat cot's long body slid past effortless
as a fish, sinewing from side to side,
as he passed us and vanished.

Philadelphia

A compound bass roar
an ocean voice
Metropolis in the ear
soft-thundered among the towers below
breaking in a hiss of detail
but without wave-rhythm
without breath-rhythm
exhalation without cease
amplified
of terrible pressure
interrupted by brief blasts and nasal shouts
guttural diesels
a sky-train waning in a line of thunder.

I opened the great atlas on the desk.

The Atlantic curved on the world.

Carraroe

Our far boundary was Gorumna island
low on the water, dotted
with granite erratics, extended grey-green
along the opposite shore of the bay
toward the south Connemara series.

On our shore, among a tumble of boulders
on the minced coral, there was one
balanced with rugged edge upward,
stuck with limpets. Over it,
with the incoming tide, the waters

wash back and forth irregularly
and cover and uncover the brown angles.
Films of liquid light run
shimmering, cut by shell-points, over
stone inclines and clotted buds of anemones.

The films fatten with plasm and flow and fill
more loosely over the rock and gradually drown it.
Then larger movements invade from further out,
from the depths,
alive and in movement. At night-time,

in the wind, at that place,
the water-wash lapped at itself under the rocks
and withdrew rustling down the invisible grains.
The ocean worked in dark masses in the bay
and applied long leverage at the shore.

*

We were finished, and quiet.
The music was over.
The lamp hissed in the tent.

We collected the cooking things
and plates and mugs and cutlery
scattered around us in the grass,
everything bone cold,
and put it all in the plastic basin.

I unhooked the lamp and made my way down
flickering over the rocks with the children
to the edge of the ocean.

[113]

A cell of light hollowed around us
out of the night. Splashes and clear voices echoed
as the spoons and knives were dug down
and enamel plates scooped under water
into the sand, and scraped and rinsed.

I held the lamp out a little over the sea.
Silvery sand-eels seethed everywhere we stepped :
shivered and panicked through the shallows,
vanished — became sand — were discovered,
picked up with exclamations,
held out damp and deathly,
little whips fainted away
in wet small palms, in an iodine smell.

*

She was standing in a sheltered angle,
urgent and quiet.
                    'Look back. . .'

The great theatre of Connemara,
dark. A cloud bank stretched in folds
across the sky, luminous
with inner activity.

Centred on the beached lamp
a single cell of cold light,
part land and part living water,
blazed with child voices.

They splashed about the stark red basin,
pouncing. They lifted it and consulted.
Their crystalline laughter escaped upward,
their shadows huge.

*

We made off toward the rocky point
past the tent's walls flapping.

A new music came on the wind : string sounds hissing
mixed with a soft inner-ear roar
blown off the ocean; a persistent
tympanum double-beat (—'darkly expressive,
coming from innermost depths. . .') That old
body music. *Schattenhaft.* SONG OF THE NIGHT. . .
A long horn call, 'a single note
that lingers, changing colour as it fades. . .'

Overhead a curlew — God in Heaven ! —
responded !
                    'poignant. . .' Yes !
'hauntingly beautiful. . .' Yes !

The bay — every inlet   lifted
and glittered toward us in articulated light.
The land, a pitch-black stage
of boulder shapes and scalps of heaped weed,
inhaled.

            A part of the mass
grated and tore, cranking harshly,
and detached and struggled upward
and beat past us along the rocks,
bat-black, heron-slow.

[115]

THE MESSENGER

1978

IN MEMORY OF
JOHN PAUL KINSELLA
DIED MAY 1976

For days I have wakened and felt immediately
half sick at something. Hour follows hour
but my shoulders are chilled with expectation.

It is more than mere Loss
                              (your tomb-image
drips and blackens, my leaden root
curled on your lap)
                              or 'what you missed'.
(The hand conceives an impossible Possible
and exhausts in mid-reach.
What could be more natural?)

Deeper. A suspicion in the bones
as though they too could melt in filth.

Something to discourage goodness.

A moist movement within.
A worm winds on its hoard.
A rim of hide lifts like a lip.

A dead egg glimmers — a pearl in muck
glimpsed only as the muck settles.
The belly settles and crawls tighter.

HIS mother's image settled on him
out of the dark, at the last,
and the Self sagged, unmanned.

Corded into a thick dressing gown
he glared from his rocker
at people *whispering* on television.

He knocked the last drops of Baby Power
into his glass and carried the lifewater
to his lips. He recollected himself

and went on with a story out of Guinness's
— the Brewery pension 'abated' by 'an amount
equal to the amount' of some pittance

on some Godforsaken pretext.
His last battle — the impulse
at its tottering extreme :

muster your fellow pensioners, and advance
pitched with them
                           ('Power to the Spent !')

against the far off boardroom door.
All about him, open mouthed,
they expired in ones and twos.

Somebody well dressed
pressed my hand in the graveyard.
A thoughtful delegated word or two :

'His father before him. . . Ah, the barge captain. . .
A valued connection. He will be well remembered. .
He lived in his two sons.'

In his own half fierce force
he lived! And stuck the first brand shakily
under that good family firm,

formed their first Union,
                          and entered their lists. . .
Mason and Knight

gave ground in twostep,
manager and priest
                    disappeared

and reappeared under each other's hats;
the lumpenproletariat
stirred truculently and settled;

in jigtime, to the ever popular
Faith Of Our Fathers, he was high and dry.
And indeed, in time, was well remembered.

In front of the fireplace, florid and with scorn,
in his frieze jacket, with a couple of bottles
of Export in the pockets, he stomached it.

Thumbs in belt, back and forth
in stiff boots he rocked with the news
(I care) (But accept) (I reject) (I do not)

in full vigour, in his fiftieth year,
every ounce of youth
absorbed into his body.

For there is really nothing to be done.
There is an urge, and it is valuable,
but it is of no avail.

He brandished his solid body
thirty feet high above their heads therefore
and with a shout of laughter

traversed a steel beam in the Racking Shed
and dared with outstretched arms
what might befall.

And it befell, that summer,
after the experimental doses,
that his bronchi wrecked him with coughs

and the muffled inner
heartstopping little
hammerblows began.

*

A brave leap   On bright prospects
in full heart   sable : a
into full stop.   slammed door.

Vaunt and check
Cursus inter-
ruptus.

[123]

TYPICALLY, there is a turning away.
The Self is islanded in fog.
It is meagre and plagued with wants

but secure. Every positive matter
that might endanger — but also enrich —
is banished. The banished matter

(a cyst, in effect, of the subject's aspirations
painful with his many disappointments)
absorbs into the psyche, where it sleeps.

Intermittently, when disturbed, it wakes
as a guardian — or 'patron' — monster
with characteristic conflicting emotional claims :

appalling, appealing; exacting sympathy
even as it threatens. (Our verb 'to haunt'
preserves the ambiguity exactly.)

Somewhere on the island, Cannibal
lifts his halved head and bellows
with incompleteness. . . Or better —

a dragon slashes its lizard wings uneasily
as it looks out and smells the fog
and itches and hungers in filth and fire.

*

Often, much too familiar for comfort,
the beast was suddenly there
insinuating between us:

'Who'd like to know what *I* know?'
'Who has a skeleton in *his* meat cupboard?'

'Who is inclined to lapse and let
the bone go with the dog?'

'Who flings off in a huff
and never counts the cost
as long as there's a bitter phrase
to roll around on the tongue?'

'When Guess Who polished his pointy shoe
and brushed his brilliantine
to whose admiring gaze
guess who hoodwinked Who?'

Or it would sigh and say:
'Guess who'd love to gobble *you* up . . . !'
Or 'Who'd like to see what *I* have?'

*

I would. . .

     And have followed
the pewtery heave of hindquarters
into the fog, the wings down at heel,

until back there in the dark
the whole thing
fell on its face.

And blackened. . . And began
melting its details and dripping them away
little by little to reveal

him (supine, jutjawed and
incommunicable, privately
surrendering his tissues and traps).

And have watched my hand reach in under
after something, and felt it
close upon it and ease him of it.

The eggseed Goodness
that is also called
Decency.

G OODNESS is where you find it.
Abnormal.
      A pearl.

A milkblue
blind orb.
      Look in it :

I T is outside the Black Lion, in Inchicore.
A young man. He is not much more than thirty.
He is on an election lorry, trying to shout.

He is goodlooking and dark.
He has a raincoat belted tight
and his hair is brushed back, like what actor. . .

He is shouting about the Blueshirts
but his voice is hoarse.
His arm keeps pointing upward.

I am there. A dark little
blackvelvet-eyed jew-child
with leaflets.

A big Dublin face
leans down with a moustache, growling
it is a scandal.

         *

The Oblate Fathers was packed.
I sat squeezed against a cold pillar.
A bull-voice rang among the arches.

An old turkey-neck in front, with a cured boil
on top of the collar, kept swallowing.
A woman whispered in my back hair.

I made faces at my ghost in the brawn marble.
The round shaft went up shining
into a mouth of stone flowers

and the angry words echoed among
the hanging lamps, off the dark golden walls,
telling every Catholic how to vote.

He covered my hand with his
and we started getting out
in the middle of Mass past everybody.

Father Collier's top half in the pulpit
in a muscular black soutane and white lace
grabbed the crimson velvet ledge

— thick white hair, glasses,
a red face, a black mouth —
shouting Godless Russia at us.

IT is an August evening, in Wicklow.
It is getting late. They have tussled in love.
They are hidden, near the river bank.

They lie face up in the grass, not touching,
head close to head, a woman and her secret husband.
A gossamer ghost arrows and hesitates

out of the reeds, and stands in the air above them
insect-shimmering, and settles on a bright
inner upturn of her dress. The wings

close up like palms. The body, a glass worm,
is pulsing. The tail-tip winces and quivers :

I *think* this is where I come in. . .

Trailing a sunless instinct,
a saw-jawed multiple past,
an edible (almost liquid)
vulnerability,
and winged! — weightless and wondrous! —
up from the bloodied slime
through the arms of a black rainbow
scooping down in beauty
he has come, he has arisen
out of the pool of night!

It is! It is!
                Hurry!
says the great womb-whisper.
Quick!
        I am all egg!

[129]

INSIDE, it is bare but dimly alive.
Such light as there is comes in overcast
through a grey lace curtain across the window,

diffuses in the dust above the bench
and shows him stooped over his last
in a cobbler's shop. He is almost still a boy :

his hands are awkwardly readying something,
his face and shoulders are soft-handsome,
pale silver, ill at ease

in the odour-bearing light. The rest is obscure,
swallowed back in man-smells
of leather and oily metal, and the faintest

musk. Beside him, his father's leaden skull
is inclined, gentle and deaf,
above the work on his apron.

The old lion-shoulders expand in the Guinness jersey,
the jaws work in his cheeks
as the quivering awl

pierces the last hole in a sole with a grunt.
He wheezes and pulls it out, and straightens.
The tide is rising and the river runs fast

into the middle span of the last bridge.
He touches the funnel on a nerve at the base
and doffs it on its hinge at the last instant

[130]

— the smoke occluding — and hauls it up again
gleaming and pluming in open water.
Here and there along the Liffey wall

he is acclaimed in friendly mockery,
humbly, saturninely, returned. . .
He reaches for needle and thread

patiently, as his son
struggles at the blank iron foot
in his father's den.

He will not stick at this. . . The knife-blades,
the hammers and pincers, the rasps and punches,
the sprigs in their wooden pits,

catching the light on the plank bench
among uppers and tongues and leather scraps
and black stumps of heelball.

He reaches for a hammer,
his jaw jutting as best it can
with Marx, Engels, Larkin

howling with upstretched arms into the teeth
of Martin Murphy and the Church
and a flourish of police batons,

Connolly strapped in a chair
regarding the guns
that shall pronounce his name for ever.

Baton struck,
             gun spat,
and Martin Murphy shall change his hat.

Son and father, upright, right arms raised.
Stretching a thread.
Trying to strike right.

DEEPER. The room where they all lived
behind the shop. It is dark here too — shut off
by the narrow yard. But it doesn't matter :

it is bustling with pleasure.
A new messenger boy
stands there in uniform, with shining belt !

He is all excitement : arms akimbo,
a thumb crooked by the telegram pouch,
shoes polished, and a way to make in the world.

His eyes are bright,
his schoolmaster's tags fresh in mind.
He has a few of the Gentlemen's Sixpenny Library

under the bed — *A Midsummer Night's Dream*,
Sartor Resartus, *The Divine Comedy*, with a notebook,
Moore's *Melodies*, a trifle shaken. . . Shelley, unbound. . .

He unprops the great Post Office bicycle
from the sewing machine and wheels it through the passage
by odours of apron and cabbage-water and whitewashed damp

through the shop and into the street.
It faces uphill. The urchin mounts. I see
a flash of pedals ! And a clean pair of heels !

A cross grain of impotent anger. About it
the iridescent, untouchable secretions
collect. It is a miracle:

membrane and mineral in precious combination.
An eye, pale with strain, forms in the dark.
The oddity nestles in slime

functionless, in all its rarity,
purifying nothing. But nothing can befoul it
— which ought probably to console.

He rolled on rubber tyres
out of the chapel door. The oak box
paused gleaming in the May morning air

and turned, sensing its direction.
Our scattered tribe began gathering itself
and trudged off onto a gravel path after it.

By their own lightness
four girls and three boys separated themselves
in a ragged band out from our dull custom

and moved up close after it, in front,
all shapes and sizes,
grandchildren, colourful and silent.

COMMENTARY

BUTCHER'S DOZEN

On the afternoon of Sunday 30 January 1972 the Dublin radio programme was interrupted by an announcement that there had been shooting at a Civil Rights demonstration in Derry, and that thirteen demonstrators had been killed by the British army. The BBC in London announced that gunmen had opened fire on the army and that bombers in the crowd had forced the troops to retaliate; there was a lot of specific detail, supplied by the army.

Official British versions of Irish events have a bad reputation — certainly in Ireland. They are meant for immediate consumption by an outside world that is ill-informed and not much concerned. It soon became clear, not least from adjustments to the official British version, that there had been a brutal and stupid massacre.* It was apparent that 'Bloody Sunday' required more than the first official response. The British Government announced the setting-up of a Tribunal of Inquiry under the Chairmanship of Lord Widgery, the Lord Chief Justice, to make a full investigation.

---

*This is not necessarily to say that it was not deliberate. Brigadier Frank Kitson in his book *Low Intensity Operations* (London 1971) in considering the army's possible contribution to combating non-violent civil action, recognises 'the simplest method of all, which is to suppress the movement by the ruthless application of naked force. . .' He acknowledges that 'although non-violent campaigns are particularly vulnerable to this sort of action, it is most unlikely that the British government, or indeed any Western government, would be politically able to operate on these lines even if it wanted to do so.' In official British thinking Northern Ireland could well constitute a special limbo in this regard, as it does in so many others.

There had been other killings in the North, but this was the first in the latest 'troubles' that involved the British army. The old combination of brutality and unruffled falsehood awoke a mass of dormant feelings in the Republic. In Dublin, thousands watched in fury and approval as the British Embassy in Merrion Square was burned down. A usually dispassionate and mocking acquaintance said : 'You forget sometimes that you hate the English.' On Sunday 6 February, one week after Bloody Sunday, thousands travelled North over the border to join a protest march in Newry, going stubbornly against the wishes of the Civil Rights organisers, who wanted no Southern Republicanism taking over their protest. The Southern contingent was careful not to offend; they were quiet and obedient, content to stare into British guns.

Witnesses before Lord Widgery included people who had been present at the demonstration, ballistics and explosives experts and the paratroopers who had done the shooting. Their evidence was not fully reported in British newspapers at the time, but it was published in great detail in Ireland, and accumulated into a clear indictment of the British troops and their officers. The Tribunal, after a brief consideration, exonerated the troops more or less, and managed to leave a suspicion of conspiracy and covert violence hanging over some of the victims. The Tribunal's Report was published for a few pence a copy; the evidence was published separately, at more than a hundred pounds. Discrepancies between the evidence and the Tribunal's findings would not therefore be immediately obvious to the casual reader.

Samuel Dash, a Philadelphia lawyer who came to international attention shortly afterward, during the Watergate investigations, reported in detail on the Tribunal's performance for the International League for the Rights of Man in New York. In his opinion

The record of the Widgery Tribunal justifies a finding that the 13 known civilian dead were unarmed when they were killed on January 30 1972 in Londonderry, and that they were shot either recklessly or deliberately by paratroopers of the First Battalion Parachute Regiment. . .

He concluded:

. . . an official inquiry which began with promise did not fulfil that promise. . . There remains the unfinished business to see that a full measure of justice is provided for those who were killed and wounded, as well as their families. Great Britain and the world cannot simply walk away from 'Bloody Sunday'.*

But they have done so. The British Ambassador to Ireland at the time, Sir John Peck, has recently published his reminiscences, dealing largely with his time in Dublin. For him the major and most dangerous event of the time was the burning of his Embassy in Dublin. He accepts the findings of the Widgery Tribunal at face value. He would accept that Bloody Sunday could have another construction put upon it, but only in 'certain circles'. I was in Philadelphia on the first anniversary of Bloody Sunday; a local group picketed the BOAC office on Kennedy Boulevard, having failed to solve the problem of picketing the British Consulate on the fifteenth floor of a nearby office block. The event was mentioned briefly on the radio, with the explanation that on Bloody Sunday the previous year a gun battle had broken out in Londonderry between the IRA and the British army and that thirteen IRA gunmen had been killed. Explanatory matter of this kind is supplied on request by the British Information Service in the United States; where else would a harrassed news editor turn,

*Justice Denied: A Challenge to Lord Widgery's Report on 'Bloody Sunday'. Published by the Defence and Education Fund of the International League for the Rights of Man, 777 United Nations Plaza, New York.

reporting on the same day the return of American troops from Vietnam? There is no Irish news agency.

Foreign ignorance of Irish matters goes deep, even where there is general sympathy. I took a taxi to the Philadelphia Airport about this time and fell into conversation with the driver. Having discovered, without much difficulty, that I was Irish, and travelling to Dublin, he told me (with all due consideration and courtesy, and making allowance for honourable exceptions) that he would be ashamed to be Irish. I asked him his origins : he was Scottish Presbyterian.

This is no place to 'set things straight'. The facts are available in any event in Liam de Paor's *Divided Ulster* (Penguin Books). And the point of view in *Butcher's Dozen* is clear enough. Though it was written in rage and haste at the time nothing has happened in the intervening six years that calls for serious revision (except possibly the 'happy ending').

Amid the swirling evils, miseries and stupidities in the North there are a few certainties :

(1) Northern Ireland is a state founded in injustice. It was established during a suspension of democratic process in Ireland — a suspension forced on the British Government by the Unionist minority. Its borders were fixed so as to contain the maximum area and resources over which that minority, on a return to democratic process, would remain a controlling majority.

(2) It is a state maintained in injustice, the artificially created anti-Unionist minority North of the border being repressed and discriminated against for more than fifty years, while successive British Governments have ignored their responsibility in the matter.

(3) Withdrawal of the British army from Northern Ireland will not of itself solve anything. But no solution is possible without its withdrawal.

Violence is terrible, but it is not inhuman. In political terms it is the final response to unredressed injustice. And no amount of opposing violence will make it go away — only the removal of its causes. The British authorities have chosen, for passing expediencies in their own 'larger' politics, to evade the treatment of awkward, deep-seated causes in Ireland. This is nothing new on their part. But it was cause for great discouragement that politics in the Republic should have returned, under the Coalition Government of the middle 1970s, to a Redmondite posture, accommodating the British authorities in their evasion. Real issues during this crucial period were narrowed or abandoned in an atmosphere of stylish debate and selective formulations uncaring of (it seemed, finally, unaware of) the realities of human behaviour. Politicians in responsible positions urged what amounted to a Violence Eradication Scheme, as though Violence were a contagious disease curable by the elimination of infected bodies. Such politicians refused to consider the eradication of the causes of violence, and attempted to prevent discussion of such causes as 'unhelpful' and 'untimely'. It is probable that some of these considerations inspired the Irish electorate in 1977 to reject emphatically a Government grown so unrepresentative.

*

Butcher's Dozen was not written in response to the shooting of the thirteen dead in Derry. There are too many dead, on all sides, and it is no use pitting them hideously against one another. The poem was written in response to the Report of the Widgery Tribunal. In Lord Widgery's cold putting aside of truth, the *n*th in a historic series of expedient falsehoods — with Injustice literally wigged out as Justice — it was evident to me that we were suddenly very close to the operations of the evil real causes.

I couldn't write the same poem now. The pressures were special, the insult strongly felt, and the timing vital if the response was to matter, in all its kinetic impurity. Reaching for the nearest aid, I found the *aisling* form — that never

[141]

quite extinct Irish political verse-form — in a late, parodied guise : in the coarse energies and nightmare Tribunal of Merriman's *Midnight Court.* One changed one's standards, chose the doggerel route, and charged. . .

The poem was finished, printed and published within a week of the publication of the Widgery Report, and I believe it had the effect I wanted, 'unhelpful' though I am sure it was. It has been criticized on various grounds, some political : it did not put adequate emphasis on the Civil Rights campaign in the North; it did not lament the 'Protestant dead' — for which I was 'lowest of the low'; it did not mention the bigotry of the Catholic Church, or the Republic's censorship laws, or the law against the open sale of contraceptives; it was presumptuous of me to deal with the Northern issue at all — living in the Republic, I had not earned the right. It was criticised also for its motives : I had written it for publicity or for money. And it was criticised for its style. It offended many *a priori* assumptions as to poetic propriety of one kind or another, as to the place of poetry in public affairs, etc.; it was unwise in its directness of response; it was not poetry at all.

I have, in fact, a few regrets. I failed to fit in a reference to the culpable silence of the Catholic Church, North and South, in the face of Northern injustice during the long build-up to the current troubles. The poem doesn't bring out properly the price paid by the Northern majority for its long, grim dominance : its mediocrity, due to the exodus of its best intelligences. And it didn't occur to me then, what seems so obvious now, how easy and helpful it would have been, and still could be, for the Protestant minority in the South to have answered the hysterical sectarian warnings from the North about the horrors of possible Southern 'Rome Rule' — to ease this central sore merely by pointing to their own comfort and privileges, as a class, in the Republic.

*

On 6 October 1971, in the small town of Coolea in West Cork, a remarkable funeral took place. From every part and every element of the country many hundreds came to take their leave of Seán O Riada, a young man who had laid extraordinary hold on their emotions.

Seán O Riada was born in Cork in 1931 and died in a London hospital on 3 October 1971. There is general agreement that he was Ireland's foremost composer and musician, but there is some argument as to the main emphasis of his career.

Measured by orthodox standards, of the publication and performance of concert works, his achievement is small: half a dozen or so works for full orchestra, of varying scope, in advanced modern idiom and of striking quality; also a group of songs and some early piano pieces. The smallness of his output was not due to any lack of attention or praise from critics — indeed, to those accustomed to think only in terms of the orchestral or chamber ensemble, O Riada's refusal to fulfil their expectations seemed baffling and frustrating — a wilful refusal to fulfil a great potential.

For O Riada, however, the traditional 'European' relationship between the composer and a select audience appears from the beginning to have been uninspiring. His escape from it may come, in time, to be seen as his biggest achievement. It came about, not through any new devices, but through his revival of the old native relationship between Irish traditional music and the Irish community, and his renovation of it for the twentieth century. This enabled him to make the whole nation his audience for a time, and to affect it deeply, without abandoning musical standards.

The power to do this came from the modern means of mass communication, but also from a unique assembly of qualities in O Riada's material, in his national audience, and in himself. His primary material was Ireland's rich store of

[143]

traditional songs and dance tunes — the music of a sophis-
ticated tradition, which he was always at pains to distinguish
from folk music as usually understood. As he found it, this
music survived in relative purity only in certain remote Irish-
speaking areas of the country; elsewhere it had been debased
to a crude popular dance music. O Riada restored life and
nobility to it by his analytic ear for its essential melodic
excellence and by his great personal gift for presentation.
Avoiding the path of concert arrangements, he founded a
group of traditional musicians, the Ceoltóirí Chualann, in a
Dublin suburb, established over them an almost hypnotic
sway, and drew from them solo and ensemble performances
that astonished even themselves. The influence of this group
was felt immediately and widely, and transformed the world
of Irish traditional music for good.

But O Riada captured his widest audience with a feat of a
different kind. In the early sixties he was commissioned to
write the music for a documentary film Mise Eire (I am
Ireland); the film was to cover Ireland's struggle for political
freedom and to reach a climax with the Easter Rebellion of
1916. Fully aware of the reserves of national feeling such a
project might draw upon, O Riada went for his main theme
to Ireland's great emblematic song of lamentation and pride,
Róisín Dubh (The Black Rose); he virtually recreated it, and
wrung from it, in full Mahlerian and Sibelian harmonies,
every emotional possibility. It is a monument to his talent
that the result, while devastating the audience for whom it
was produced, remains a fine musical achievement.

Further concerts and recordings with the Ceoltóirí Chual-
ann, and other film music (some with the Ceoltóirí), accounted
for a great deal of O Riada's last ten years. His most recent
new work in music was the writing of a simple Mass for the
people of the Irish-speaking parish of Coolea, where he settled
down in 1964. This represented, of course, an even closer
relationship between music and the community, but it is
impossible to say what it would have come to, musically,

[144]

given time to develop — as it is impossible to say more of the country's loss by his early death than that it is great, and gravely felt.

T. K.

from *Eire/Ireland*, Bulletin of the Department of Foreign Affairs, Dublin : 14 January 1972.

*

Ceoltóirí Laighean number among them some of the very finest individual performers of Irish traditional music and song, as The Star of Munster *amply testifies. But they are even more important, as a group, for the ideal they represent, blending their talents in the lively expression of a noble tradition. The founding of Ceoltóirí Laighean in 1972 was a responsible act on the part of Eamon de Buitléar, who is trying to carry on what can be carried on of Seán O Riada's work.*

de Buitléar was an important member of O Riada's pioneering and influential group, Ceoltóirí Chualann, and remains committed to O Riada's aims — which went beyond the mere presentation of Irish music to a larger audience than it had ever had. He was in fact uniquely helpful to O Riada in the early 1960s in gathering the original musicians together. One of them was the Clare fiddler John Kelly who, with his knowledge of traditional tunes and local styles, became O Riada's guide into a virtually hidden world. John Kelly has keen memories of how traditional musicians were regarded up to that time, and as keen a sense of the dignity O Riada restored to them.

O Riada's decision to move from Dublin to Cúil Aodha in West Cork in 1964 put a certain strain on Ceoltóirí Chualann. They gathered for particular occasions but, for continuity and the fuller use of their talents, a number of them assembled together under the great piper Paddy Moloney as The Chieftains. *The Chieftains—the first offshoot of O Riada's work — have since developed their own style, using all O*

[145]

Riada's discoveries and inventions, and many of the tunes he revived (and composed), exploiting the music for sheer entertainment.

But for O Riada the music was as much a means as an end in itself, a means towards cultural integration; language, song and music fitted into, and fulfilling, a way of life. It is an ideal, requiring a very special community (at times, in Cúil Aodha, it seems close at hand . . .) and it is this ideal that brought Ceoltóirí Laighean into being — to realise, in music and song, whatever of it is possible.

T. K.

from the record sleeve for *The Star of Munster* — Gael-Linn : 1975.

*

This music is the last that Seán O Riada was concerned with. He had the tape with him in London during his last illness, and he seemed to cling to life with it. Listening with him to the unedited version, punctuated by his recorded voice in occasional vigorous comment, was a strange and painful experience.

In a full musical career, this record might seem an entertainment by the way, a charming personal flourish. As things happened, it must do duty as O Riada's farewell; it does so with elegance and appropriateness.

His more notable achievements in music have always involved others — the musicians and poets of the Gaelic past, his own Ceoltóirí, his adopted community in Coolea. These achievements, despite their communal aspect, were truly individual; like all art they stemmed from one tragically perishable talent. It is appropriate that O Riada's last offering should be not only traditional but a display of individual mastery.

T. K.

from the record sleeve note for *O Riada's Farewell* — Claddagh Records : 1972.

John Reidy was introduced to a number of us in Dublin in 1951, in the students' restaurant in 86 St. Stephen's Green. He had finished his degree in music in University College, Cork, and was in Dublin for an interview. He was pale and thin, and playful under scrutiny. He laid claim to absolute pitch and, by suggestion, to absolute knowledge in musical matters. Two musicians in the company tested him and swiftly revealed their limitations. His use of a Latin quotation was matched by another, but he shook off pursuit with something in Greek that sounded fluent and convincing. His French sounded excellent; it certainly impressed two girls who were taking their M.A. in French. Someone from Trim was trying to define existentialism; he set the definition right. Likewise with progressive jazz: he was dogmatic about Jerry Mulligan and George Shearing. He had played the jazz piano himself, professionally. . .

I was working in the Department of Finance at the time. I must have been on leave that day, because I remember sitting on with Reidy when the others had left, dabbing out butts in a wet saucer. I forget most of what we talked about, but I remember enjoying his company and being drawn to him by the recognition that our minds shared an odd blend of rigour and squalor. We had earlier dismissed without much discussion the whole mentality of the 'L & H' — the Literary and Historical Society at U.C.D.: all syllogisms, debating brilliance and commanding mannerisms. Now we were pleased to discover a common interest in science fiction. We were in agreement on the merits of Hal Clements, whose *Mission of Gravity* was just then appearing in serial form in *Astounding*. Reidy had read Olaf Stapledon and we agreed on his importance.

We walked that evening by the canal and along the South Circular Road toward Dolphin's Barn, where he confessed that he believed in ghosts — he had actually heard one approaching him, opening and closing door after door, down the corridors of a deserted hotel in Valentia. I told him that

[147]

I believed in God, and he was interested but puzzled. He went back to Cork next day.

He had been in Dublin trying for a job as Assistant Director of Music in Radio Eireann. He was soon notified that he had been successful and he wrote to say he was coming to Dublin to look for a place to live. Early one afternoon I was talking to a visitor in the lobby of the Department of Finance in Merrion Street, at the side window overlooking the grounds of the Natural History Museum. Looking out on the summer sunshine, I noticed that people going in the direction of Clare Street were staring at something. An extraordinary, sombre figure came into view : it was Reidy, with death-white face, in a long black tight overcoat, with black umbrella, black beret, gloves and scarf. He turned in at the Department steps and I watched him through the glass partition being ushered into the waiting room, where he sat erect and expressionless on the edge of the seat, the umbrella held upright in front of him. The porter nodded to me, smiling unsurely.

He had returned, and he was here to ask if he might stay in Baggot Street with me while the search for his own place proceeded. He went off to meet some people from Radio Eireann, and didn't arrive at the flat until very late. He slept on the floor, and was still asleep when I left for the office next morning. At lunchtime, when I looked in, he was beginning to stir. He seemed to expect breakfast. I left him to fend for himself and didn't see him until late that evening. He had met a few people from Radio Eireann and had done nothing about finding a place. He would give up to-morrow to that.

We listened to some records on a record player I was buying — a real extravagance. The sounds were clean and wonderful : Bach's cello suites, the *Orgelbuechlein* . . . a refreshing rigour. But also Sibelius's Second Symphony, with the long excitations and glittering elephantine climax of the finale. . .

We talked until very late, in various accents. Reidy was very good at American, and also at a glutinous Balkan voice.

[148]

He had a great store of good dirty stories. He retired to the floor and we intoned Wordsworth's sonnet *Upon Westminster Bridge* antiphonally, in BBC voices.

Next morning he slept late again. As I left for the Department I pulled the curtains back to let in the light. I didn't call in at lunch time and when I came home at five o'clock he was gone. I worked a little and made a pot of tea, and sat reading. He came in late and said he had had no luck with the search; no one he met knew anything about an available place. I asked had he looked at the small ads in the newspapers. He hadn't, but he would try the next day.

It lasted a week. One night, as he hovered over my bookshelves, I ran my eye down the advertisements in the evening paper and picked out an item almost at random. It was in Lower Mount Street, on the corner facing Clanwilliam House. It was fairly expensive for what it was (a dark rat-trap partitioned off a back landing). I told him it was a rare opportunity, so central, and not to be missed. He moved in at once.

He too bought a record player. He had access to Radio Eireann's entire record library and brought many records home with him. I remember the elaborate, opulent close of *Der Rosenkavalier* filling the mean little space : the unmade single bed, the dusty electric fire glowing in the grate, spattered with butts, Reidy's narrow, unfocussed face intent in the dark like an animal. I heard Mahler there for the first time. Reidy played *Das Lied von der Erde* again and again. And Jerry Mulligan, and George Shearing.

When it was time for regression, and squallor came uppermost, we would cruise the dark streets looking for a little harmless evil, ineffectual, like a pair of ill-matched adolescents. We sat drinking coffee late one night in a gaunt night-place on the quays. The air was smoky, the board floor bare and unswept, the atmosphere cavernous and ugly. Someone was 'vamping' at the piano and Reidy complained so much I suggested he do something about it. He was a moder-

[149]

ately good player but always very reluctant, because he liked to grow his fingernails very long, and they scraped when he played. But the idea of the gesture tempted him. He went up to the pianist and asked to play, then sat down and tore off the tops of his nails and played for a quarter of an hour to the admiration of the surrounding tables.

The first drunken evening I recall was spent with some journalists in a pub called *The Kind Ladies*, a dreary den in a street of warehouses somewhere behind Amiens Street. We were a pair of simple and lonely seamen from the Baltic, and were made welcome as such. We made monosyllabic attempts at communication with the inhabitants, in soft expletives, and there was a lot of laughter. The circular table was crowded with glasses and opened bottles; dregs and floating ash washed about.

He married shortly after, and he and Ruth stayed in a flat in Merrion Square, which gave them access to the Square itself, then closed to the public. He assembled a model airplane and flew it there, chasing it across the unkempt grass in his long open black overcoat, as it crashed again and again until it could fly no more.

Sometimes he would talk obsessively about his musical plans. There were to be a number of orchestral suites that he called 'nomoi', one in particular to be a huge choral work using choruses from Sophocles. I knew his working method and his short attention span, and would have laid odds against these works being completed. But they all were, sooner or later.

The first pieces to emerge were for piano. They were very short, and made up of tiny units. He played one at a lunchtime concert in Trinity College. It had a series of glissandi at one point running up the entire keyboard : there were at least half a dozen of these one after the other, identical, and separated by dead rests. The sparse audience could scarcely believe its ears. About the same time he gave a radio talk in his British accent. This too was excruciating. At the time he was gruffly determined about it, but he destroyed the recording afterwards and all evidence of the episode, and winced at any mention of it. He was also starting to write a few settings of Irish airs, very direct and 'intelligent'. I believe there is absolute intelligence, as there is absolute pitch, and that Reidy had it. But the playfulness of his mind had not begun to find vent in his work.

*

In 1959 we arranged for our two young families to go together on holidays to Ballyferriter in West Kerry. A former teacher of Reidy's, Father Tadhg O Murchadha, had built a summer school in An Gráig and we could stay there until the students came.

I was delayed in Dublin for a week. At the end of the week I got the train to Tralee, then a bus to Dingle, where Reidy was waiting to take me on the last stage to An Gráig. He was very excited : he had found great singers and music, Jerry Flaherty and Seán de Hóra, in Kruger Kavanagh's pub in Dunquin, and we must go and hear them straight away.

The porch of Kruger's was full of upturned barrels with a few people sitting on them. The interior of the shop was dark and cool, murmurous, and filled with presences. Reidy went up to the bar and bought drinks for everyone in the shop and chatted them all, using a very sketchy Irish but doing so unabashed, mimicking fluency. It was clear he had established himself as a character over the past week, and not only in the realm of pub talk : he was committing himself to fairly serious schemes, to using his influence in Dublin to get a fishmeal plant for the district, and grants for greenhouses for commercial tomato growing.

A voice from a dark corner near the fireplace began to sing. The song was *Casadh an tSúgáin* and the singer Jerry Flaherty. I had heard the *sean nós*, or old style, of traditional singing before, without being attracted by the raw Oriental tonalities or the nasalised, strangulated delivery. For whatever reasons, the effect was different now. Nothing intervened between the song and its expression. The singer managed many difficult things, but the result was to focus attention on the song, not on the performance or on the quality of the voice. It was a special voice, adapted (like a reptile or an insect) to its function. Mere beauty of tone would have distracted, attracting attention for its own sake. And the singer's act of communication was thoroughly completed by his audience. They sat erect and listened, lifted their glasses and drank, and murmured phrases of appreciation. When the song ended there was a slight increase in the volume of general approbation but very little fuss. Something had been accomplished, and the entities which had combined to accomplish it separated and began to chat, in the smells of fish, rope, tobacco and porter.

I was introduced and welcomed. I met the singer, Jerry Flaherty, most courteous, but untalkative. He was a fisherman and farmer like most of the local people, with a wide-cheeked lipless face like a cobra, and black slit eyes shaded under his cap. I met his friend Seán de Hóra also, small and erect-necked, most correct and polite. And Kruger Kavanagh himself, the publican, with his square clipped head, and his elbow on the counter, emphatic and confiding. ('Schubert? I knew Schubert. A great man. I worked with him in America : Boston and Philadelphia and Springfield, Massachussetts. I went ahead to the next town and did the publicity for all his concerts.') He turned to get a bottle, pivoting on his bent little finger. His heavy body moved independently in the receptacle of his great frieze trousers.

Outside, the Blasket Islands crouched on the water. We walked back toward An Gráig. As the road rounded a headland of scraggy shale the scene opened toward Ballyferriter, on a landscape of immense depth and volume, like nothing I had ever seen before. On the right, the flank of Croagh-marhin receded for miles. To the left, the fields sloped down to the bay at Clochar; foam like ragged lace crawled and gleamed rangerously in the Blasket Sound, where remnants

[152]

of the Armada still lie wrecked. In the centre, a range of headlands poured westward out to the ocean like huge breakers; on one of them, above a low cliff, were the ruins of the poet Piaras Feiritéar's castle. In the distance Mount Brandon closed the scene, the holy mountain of Saint Brendan the Navigator, with a narrow creek somewhere at its base, An Cuas, where his great voyage began to the unknown Western world. Dead centre in this prospect, under a sky full of oceanic movement, at the foot of an extraordinary little hill crested with a cock's comb of shattered rock, was our home : An tAthair Tadhg's hostel, a two-story concrete box starting up naked out of the ground, sharp-gabled and drain-piped.

We spent a couple of weeks there, the two families passing their time in separate ways. Reidy was usually in Kruger's, where he was beginning to pace his pints with glasses of Paddy or vodka. He and I went shrimping together a lot of the time, catching the tiny monsters singly with the childrens' pinkeen nets, the little grey phantoms cloudily 'cycling' (as Reidy called it) alongside the dark boatslip at Smerwyck. I enjoyed the long stress-free days and read science fiction and Wodehouse and some of the Irish books lying about the hostel. There were three issues of the folklore journal *Béaloideas*, from the 1930s, containing a long work by An Seabhac on the place-names of the Dingle peninsula. Reidy and I were fascinated by this, and 'did' the places between Dunquin and Ballyferriter. I had encountered An Seabhac in school, as the author of *Jimín Máire Thaidhg*, simple funny stories of a young boy's growing up in the Gaeltacht at the turn of the century. Now 'The Hawk' took on new flesh : an enthusiast, a teacher and researcher, heroic with notebook and bicycle clips, ranging the landscape I could feel coming to life around us.

For Reidy it was all a swift liberation, as he drove off toward Kruger's in Dunquin or O Catháin's in Ballyferriter, bustling with business, chatting and joking with the people,

[153]

exchanging songs and stories, charming and impressing them, pitching himself forward into the language with predatory energy in a spate of new ideas. As we threw ourselves down again on the slip at Smerwyck, our heads over the edge, looking into the dark water, the childrens' nets dipping toward their prey on their long canes, he turned and said : 'I feel as if I have never done anything else in my life.'

Every night there was music and singing somewhere. And always drink. We threw a party in the hostel at the end of our stay. 'Iron lungs' full of stout stood on trestles in a shed, benches were arranged along the walls, Seán de Hóra played his melodeon in the corner. It went on until almost dawn : the last to leave were de Hóra and Jerry Flaherty, walking homeward together toward Clochar in their familiar setting of slopes and headlands, luminous growling ocean and apocalyptic Western sky.

We didn't see them again until the following September, when they came to see the final at Croke Park and to make a few trial recordings for Gael-Linn. In Reidy's house in Galloping Green they spoke of the good fishing season that was just starting : after years elsewhere the big mackerel shoals had come back and they were anxious to get home and make the most of it. The next Sunday I picked up the paper and saw a photograph of an upturned black skin-boat on the quay at Dingle, and a great heap of mackerel, still tangled in the torn net. Jerry Flaherty and two others were missing; they were never found. Two of his songs had been recorded, one — *An Seanduine* — was issued by Gael-Linn as a single 78; the other — *Casadh an tSúgáin* — was unsatisfactory in some way and never issued.

Reidy's liberation continued. He pursued the schemes and the grants, and I believe that some of his ideas did lead to something. But a profounder consequence of our holiday, of course, was his unabated new drive toward Irish music. It was a recovery, in fact : he had only to become conscious of it to realise that he was already in possession of it, from the time

[154]

he played the traditional fiddle as a young boy growing up in Bruff, County Limerick, where his father had been a police sergeant. He was rapidly setting something free in himself, with all the intelligence and playfulness of which he was capable.

*

In *A Selected Life*, in the first part of section (ii), the circumstances are as 'given' : things noted during a short walk away from the crowds in the O Riada household on the morning of the funeral — rain, the crow, the coarse bell sounding across open country. It was only afterwards that I was struck by the parallels with the well-known lines from 'Marbhna Oiliféir Grás' by Seán mac Bháitéir Breathnach :

> Tá cling na marbh leis an ngaoith,
> Monuar! is teachta bróin dúinn í!
> Tá an fiach dubh le glór garbh
> Ag fógradh uaire an duine mhairbh.

> (The clang for the dead is on the wind,
> our messenger of grief, alas!
> The raven with a rough voice
> announces the dead man's hour.)

Parts of *A Selected Life* are saturated in alcohol. . . O Riada was a reasonably moderate drinker until his late twenties, but then his metabolism seemed to accelerate, and he drank heavily. I have known others, and know some still, who could drink more than he did, but I have never known anyone with the same destructive affinity for alcohol. In the last ten years of his life he aged quickly, so that in his middle thirties he looked to be about sixty. One night, when he was in

[155]

hospital in London, I brought something he had asked for earlier in the day : the night nurse let me in with great reluctance, and the warning : 'Remember, he is a very old man.'

The genesis of *Vertical Man* is the strangest of any poem I have written. The September after O Riada's death I was back in Philadelphia after more than a year's absence in Dublin. I brought O Riada's death mask with me, and a cast of his left hand. A few weeks after my return, after a day spent working on poems from a long sequence and on *The Good Fight*, I started unpacking old books and records in my apartment. While I dusted them and arranged them in their places I played a few records. I came upon the record *Vertical Man*, with O Riada's photograph on the sleeve, sitting in his waistcoat, with cigar, and quizzical face averted, dangling a lay figure in front of him with surreptitious obscenity. I propped the record sleeve against the bookcase, under the death mask and the hand, making a little altar. I finished the tidying, and picked out *Das Lied von der Erde.* I poured a glass of Bourbon and stood proposing a toast to the picture, the death mask and the hand. Out in the city darkness there was a sudden terrifying amplified screaming. I filled with panic — being still unaccustomed, after my long absence, to the alarums of the fire station around the corner in Market Street. I relaxed and drank, and then O Riada's presence was in the room; for an extraordinary moment we drank together. Then the presence went off into the darkness. It was a definite farewell. It is the only experience of the kind I have had, and it occurred on the first anniversary of O Riada's death.

On the second and third pages of the poem offerings are being made to the ghost, in propitiation : two sentences from Plato's *The Laws*, from among the drafts of *The Good Fight*, and the 'plot' of the long sequence I had been working on during the day.

The closing section of *Vertical Man*, apart from the last three quatrains, is based on the poem used by Gustav Mahler

in the opening movement of *Das Lied von der Erde*. The text
of the poem, *Das Trinklied vom Jammer der Erde* by Hans
Bethge, is as follows :

Schon winkt der Wein im gold'nen Pokale,
Doch trink noch nicht, erst sing ich euch ein Lied!
Das Lied vom Kummer soll auflachend
In die Seele euch klingen. Wenn der Kummer naht,
Liegen wüst die Gärten der Seele,
Welkt hin und stirbt die Freude, der Gesang.
Dunkel ist das Leben, ist der Tod.

Herr dieses Hauses!
Dein Keller birgt die Fülle des goldenen Weins!
Hier diese Laute nenn ich mein!
Die Laute schlagen und die Gläser leeren,
Das sind die Dinge, die zusammenpassen.
Ein voller Becher Wein zur rechten Zeit
Ist mehr wert als alle Reiche dieser Erde.
Dunkel ist das Leben, ist der Tod.

Das Firmament blaut ewig, und die Erde
Wird lange feststehn und aufblühn im Lenz.
Du aber, Mensch, wie lange lebst denn du?
Nicht hundert Jahre darfst du dich ergötzen
An all dem morschen Tande dieser Erde!

Seht dort hinab!
Im Mondschein auf den Gräbern hockt
Eine wild-gespenstiche Gestalt. Ein Aff ist's!
Hört ihr, wie sein Heulen hinausgellt
In den süssen Duft des Lebens!
Jetzt nehmt den Wein! Jetzt ist es Zeit, Genossen!
Leert eure goldnen Becher zu Grund!
Dunkel ist das Leben, ist der Tod.

Vertical Man is the title chosen by Seán O Riada for the Claddagh Records recording of a number of his songs and the orchestral *Hercules Dux Ferrariae*. It appears to have been taken from the following dedicatory verse in W. H. Auden's *Poems* (1930):

> *To Christopher Isherwood*
>
> Let us honour if we can
> The vertical man
> Though we value none
> But the horizontal one.

*

THE GOOD FIGHT

With the death of Kennedy many things died, foolish expectations and assumptions, as it now seems. I began the poem soon after the assassination — with how many other poems written for a while, as people roamed the nights to relieve themselves of obscure pressures. But the poem jammed and allowed time for the foolishness to digest. A great deal of foreign matter was lifted from it, and developed into a separate poem, *Worker in Mirror, at His Bench*.

In section I the speeches are made up partly of quotations from various Kennedy speeches, interviews and articles. The opening of the first speech, on page 38, is taken from a contemporary song, 'The New Frontier'; there are also sentences from Plato's *The Republic*. The italicised passages on pages 37, 40 and 41 consist mainly of quotations from Plato's *The Republic* and *The Laws*.

Elsewhere in section I and in section III individual images and phrases are taken from *The Making of the President 1960* by Theodore H. White (New York, 1961), *The Kennedy Promise* by Henry Fairlie (London, 1973), and contemporary news reports.

In section II part of the psychological argument is borrowed from 'The Silence of Oswald', an article by John Clellon Holmes in *Playboy*, November 1965. The article assumes Oswald's guilt in the assassination, and this assumption is accepted for the purpose in hand. Many of the images, and two short passages *verbatim* (the suicide vision and the final note) are taken from Oswald's own 'Historic Diary'. The passages in bold type towards the end of the section are selected, again, from Plato.